THE CAMERA
AND THE
TSARS

The last Tsar, Nicholas II, and his son Alexei in the old palace at Livadia in the Crimea, September 1909.

THE CAMERA AND THE TSARS

The Romanov Family in Photographs

CHARLOTTE ZEEPVAT

SUTTON PUBLISHING

First published in 2004 by
Sutton Publishing Limited · Phoenix Mill
Thrupp · Stroud · Gloucestershire · GL5 2BU

British Library Cataloguing in Publication Data
A catalogue record for this book is available from the British Library.

ISBN 0 7509 3049 7

Typeset in 13/18pt Bembo.
Typesetting and origination by
Sutton Publishing Limited.
Printed in Great Britain by
J.H. Haynes & Co. Ltd, Sparkford, England.

Contents

	Introduction	vii
1	The Last Tsar	1
2	The Family	21
3	Marrying into the Family	39
4	Born Romanov	57
5	The Training of Princes	75
6	A Suitable Marriage	93
7	Family Ties	111
8	The Family at Work	133
9	The Family at Play	151
10	The Passing of Tsars	173
11	War and Revolution	191
12	Full Circle	209
	Family Trees	229
	Notes	233
	Acknowledgements and List of Photographers	235
	Index	237

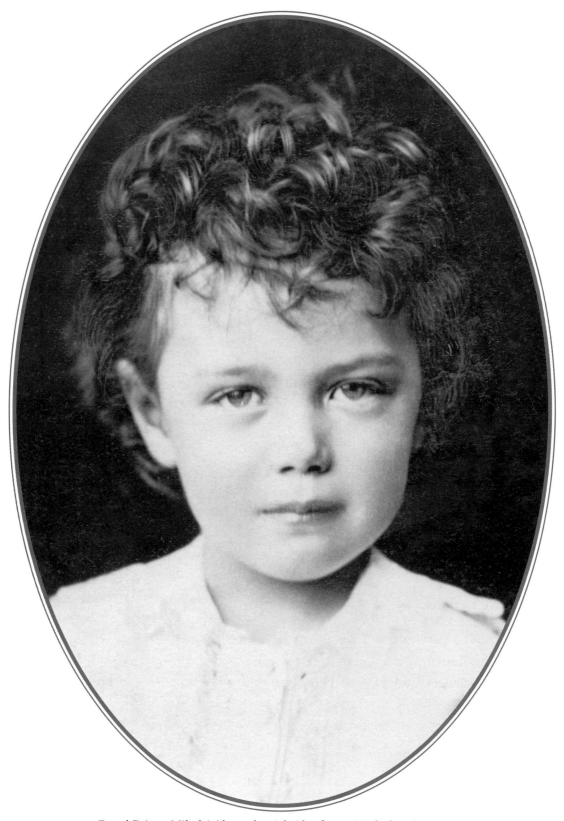

Grand Prince Nikolai Alexandrovich (the future Nicholas II) in 1870.

Introduction

You are looking into the face of a child, making eye contact across the centuries. You see the play of light on his eyes, his lashes, the patterning of the iris. He is serious, intent – perhaps a little questioning. Yet because this is a particular child – the child who will one day grow into Nicholas II, last Tsar of Russia – there is a historical irony at play here. You are aware of his future, he is not, and you are meeting him at a moment when the tragedy of the revolutionary years was beyond imagining. It might still have been prevented. He stares into the camera lens over 130 years ago. The camera and the photographer are long gone but the child lives on, his gaze captured on a frail piece of paper as if it were here and now.

Photography *is* magic. We are too familiar with it now to remember, but his generation saw the wonder and the power of a photograph. The Russian writer E.M. Almedingen recalled a story told to her by Mademoiselle Röhmer, a retired maid-of-honour from the Court of Alexander II. There was a summer party one day in the gardens at Tsarskoe Selo and the Tsar came outside and sat on the ground, relaxing with some of his guests. 'Suddenly Mademoiselle Röhmer heard steps behind her, turned and saw a man she knew – with "a marvellous apparatus" in his hands. He whispered to her. "Please say nothing. I hope I may succeed. Nobody has ever seen his Majesty at such ease." "And there was a picture taken," concluded Mademoiselle Röhmer, "and fortunately we persuaded the man to have it destroyed. . . . It was a sacrilege – to have caught his Imperial Majesty laughing, seated on the grass."'[1] In the 1850s, they understood. The camera was 'a marvellous apparatus' and to take so real a picture of a Tsar, in all his humanity, amounted to a sacrilege.

The new science – or art – of photography stirred excitement in Russia from the beginning.[2] It was on 4 January 1839, four days before the announcement of Louis Daguerre's invention at the Academy of Science in Paris, that *Severnaia Pchela*, St Petersburg's most popular newspaper, first described the daguerreotype. The newspaper saw photography as a practical tool with no artistic possibilities. But the rival *St Petersburg Gazette* correctly predicted that, in time, the photograph would become invaluable to travellers and artists alike; as more details of the discovery emerged, the pace of debate quickened. The Imperial Academy of Science sent a man named Hammel to western Europe to find out as much as possible about both of the new photographic processes: that of Daguerre, in which a unique image was produced and fixed on a treated metal plate, and the 'photogenic drawing' of Henry Fox Talbot in England, which used chemically sensitised paper. Hammel went first to England. By May his descriptions of Fox Talbot's method, together with samples of the photographer's work and materials, had reached Russia. The Academy ordered its own experiments but was not satisfied with the results; nonetheless that summer samples of Fox Talbot's sensitised paper began to be sold in the English bookshop in St Petersburg.

Hammel moved on to France, meeting Daguerre and Isidore Niépce, the son of Daguerre's deceased partner Joseph, whom Hammel came to regard as the true inventor of photography. Niépce gave him a camera (some months before these were available commercially) and Hammel sent it back to the Academy. In October 1839 the Academy of Arts in St Petersburg staged an exhibition of daguerreotypes: *Severnaia Pchela* told its readers that new daguerreotype images were being displayed every day in 'the premises of the optician and physicist Schedel'.[3] Within months the first commercial daguerreotype studios had opened in Russia and what had started as a scientific curiosity soon became a popular craze. Through the 1840s portrait studios multiplied across the country and still were barely able to meet the demand.

But what did the imperial family make of photography? At the start of 1839 Nicholas I was Tsar, having reigned for a little over thirteen years; he was also head of the Imperial Academy of Science. He was happily married to a German princess, who had taken the name Alexandra Feodorovna on Orthodox baptism. Of their seven surviving children the eldest, the Tsesarevich Alexander, was nearly twenty-one and in Italy, making the tour of Europe which would complete his education and, if all went to plan, find him a suitable wife. His sister Maria, at nineteen, was preparing for marriage to Duke Maximilian of Leuchtenberg; the younger daughters, Olga and Alexandra, and sons Konstantin, Nikolai and Mikhail were children still. The Tsar also had a brother, Grand Prince Mikhail Pavlovich, based in St Petersburg with his wife and three daughters; their two surviving sisters lived in Germany and the Netherlands. This was the imperial family in 1839. In 1841 the Tsesarevich married and by the mid-1840s there were grandchildren in direct line to the throne. In October 1843 Karl Dauthendey, a German, arrived in St Petersburg with a personal recommendation to the Imperial Court from the Duke of Anhalt-Dessau, whose family he had captured on daguerreotypes. Dauthendey worked in the Russian capital until 1862, but there is no evidence of his having taken photographs of Nicholas I's family.

The earliest surviving daguerreotypes of the imperial family, taken from life, date from the end of the 1840s. The State Hermitage in St Petersburg owns two: one of Nicholas I and one of his eldest daughter, Grand Princess Maria Nikolaevna, taken by unknown photographers. There may have been other early photographs which have not survived – daguerreotypes or paper prints, made using the calotype process invented by Fox Talbot in the autumn of 1840. The calotype was printed from a paper negative, making repeated copies possible, and from the very beginning a social distinction existed between the practitioners of the two different forms of photography. The daguerreotype was seen as a commercial product and its maker a tradesman, while the calotype process appealed more to the gentleman amateur; some refused to regard the daguerreotype as a photograph at all. But both processes were used in royal circles. The first images from life of the British royal family – daguerreotype and calotype – were taken in the 1840s. In the autumn of 1845 Nicholas I's brother-in-law Prince Wilhelm of Prussia had daguerreotypes made of himself and his children. But Nicholas may not have cared much for photography beyond its novelty value: his interests inclined always to the past. He was also a keen patron of the arts. The miniature watercolour portrait was fashionable in Russia at this time and the Tsar was both generous to his artists and knowledgeable about their work – he may not have wished to encourage an invention that would threaten their future. A year after the Tsar's death the prominent art critic Vladimir Stasov dismissed photography as a mechanical novelty, devoid of the higher qualities inherent in true art: Stasov would later change his mind, but Nicholas may well have agreed with this original opinion.

But by the mid-1850s the imperial family and the camera had embarked on a long and fruitful relationship. Nicholas died in February 1855. The Royal Collection in Windsor holds a daguerreotype of him on his deathbed which has deteriorated badly. Its provenance is unknown and it is a curious item to find in this particular collection for, at the time of the Tsar's death, England and Russia were at war. There are photographs in Russian collections of Alexander II and his children also dating from around this time, mostly taken by Andrei Denier, one of the leading Russian portrait photographers. The second half of the decade also saw the advent of the carte-de-visite photograph: a small paper print mounted on card, about the size of a visiting card. These were cheap to produce in quantity and sparked a collecting boom across Europe. The Paris firm Verry produced cartes of Alexander II, his Empress, Maria Alexandrovna, and their eldest son Nikolai, which are noticeably earlier than more familiar photographs of them. They certainly date from the mid-1850s, probably 1856, the year of Alexander's coronation, when the Armistice which ended the Crimean War was signed in Paris.

Cartes-de-visite and the larger 'cabinet' photographs, which appeared in the 1860s, would have been the first photographic likenesses of the imperial family available to the Russian people and, as the years passed, their numbers increased. While some photographs were kept within the family, to be given to friends, displayed in frames or preserved in the albums which began to be kept in Alexander II's time, card-mounted photographs were also a commercial product and none was more appealing than an image of royalty. Ordinary people wanted to own them. Photographers were given permission to sell them and they used the mounts to boast of the prizes they had won in international competition, and of their titled customers. They displayed photographs in their studio windows. In 1859 the Astronomer Royal for Scotland, Charles Piazzi Smyth, visited Russia and would later recall, 'Someone had told us on board ship that photography was miserable and hardly known in St Petersburg: that was nevertheless a decided mistake for there is scarcely a more frequent sign to be met with along all the principal streets than Photographer; and all the specimens exhibited outside the studios, chiefly large signed portraits, were among the finest things that we have ever seen in that line.'[4] In 1880 the writer Fyodor Dostoevsky was introduced to the Tsarevna Maria Feodorovna, Alexander II's daughter-in-law, at a charity evening, without being told her true identity. His daughter wrote that 'he was somewhat embarrassed that he had not recognised the Tsarevna, of whom photographs hung in all the shop windows'.[5]

Through the second half of the century photographers vied for imperial patronage. Sergei Levitsky, a trained lawyer, started taking photographs in the early 1840s and is said to have begun working for the imperial family soon after the opening of his St Petersburg studio in 1849. Over forty years later he was still taking photographs for the Tsar. Nicholas II paid him for 283 family photographs in 1896, and on 3 May of that year recorded in his diary, 'At 2.15 p.m. we went to Levitsky's son to be photographed, because the old man was ill. Various photographs were taken: the two of us with my daughter, the two of us together and on my own.'[6] Andrei Denier graduated from the St Petersburg Academy of Arts in 1851 – many of the early photographers were trained artists – and in 1865 produced the first instalment of his *Album of Photographic Portraits of August Personages and Well-Known Individuals in Russia*. There were twelve photographs in each monthly part and the series proved so popular it was extended into a second year. Denier was the first photographer to exhibit his work at the Academy of Arts. An H. Denier working for the imperial family in the 1870s and also describing himself as 'Artist' may well have been his son. Some photographers tried to catch the imperial eye with presentation albums, either of portraits, like William Carrick's series of street traders and hawkers which he gave to the Tsesarevich Nikolai in the early 1860s, or of views. An album of Andrei Karelin's photographs of Nizhni Novgorod was specially prepared for Alexander II with hand colouring by Ivan Shishkin, who became a prominent member of the 'Itinerant' group of artists and remains one of the best-loved of Russian landscape painters.

Some photographers worked their way through the ranks. W. Jasvoin's photographic mounts from the 1870s claim the patronage of Grand Prince Nikolai Nikolaevich, Alexander II's brother. In those days Jasvoin had two studios in the city, neither in a particularly good location, and in summer he followed the Court to Peterhof. By the 1890s, however, his mounts tell a different story, with the arms of 'His Imperial Majesty Emperor Alexander III, His Imperial Majesty Nikolai Alexandrovich and Her Imperial Majesty Maria Feodorovna, their Highnesses Grand Princes Vladimir, Alexei and Sergei Alexandrovich' and a fashionable address on the Grand Morskaya. Similarly, A.A. Pasetti's early mounts boasted of his work for Grand Princess Alexandra Iosifovna only, while in later years he was employed by all branches of the family; later still, under the ownership of the Swiss photographers Boissonas & Eggler, his former studio took the most familiar Romanov photographs of all – the Tercentenary series of Nicholas and Alexandra and their children.

The impression given of the family by the early photographs, up to the 1870s, was usually quite intimate. Though the majority were taken in the studio and long exposure times made a truly relaxed photograph impossible, most were posed quite naturally. Alexander II liked to be photographed with one of his dogs, usually the black labrador 'Milord'. Though always in uniform, he rarely donned orders and medals for the camera. Maria Alexandrovna was pictured working on her embroidery or posing with their children, and the children's portraits often included toys. It was left to later generations to capture the splendour of the Imperial Court – the Tsar in all his wealth and power, reviewing his armies or meeting other world leaders; the Empresses in full Court dress, decked out with a dragon's hoard of jewellery. These grand photographs were intended for public consumption: advances in camera technology meant that from the late 1880s many members of the family had their own cameras and the private snapshot took over from the studio portrait in the family albums.

Cabinet and carte-de-visite images released for exhibition or sale were reproduced in quantity but they were still real photographic prints and their circulation was limited. But by the 1890s new printing technology allowed photographic illustrations to be used in books and magazines and on picture postcards, vastly increasing the numbers of people who could enjoy them. And since, within Russia at least, it was not possible for anyone to capture an unguarded photo of the Tsar, we have to assume that the photographs that were published represent the imperial family as they wanted to be seen. Later generations of Romanovs did not rely on the moral pressure of a Mademoiselle Röhmer to control the 'marvellous apparatus'. By the end of the nineteenth century photography on the streets – even access to the transport system for a would-be photographer – was strictly controlled by police permit. Even the photographer Alexander Yagelsky, who worked under the studio name of K.E. de Hahn and had been taking photographs at Court since 1891, was refused a permit to take photographs at the 1896 coronation. The Police Department had found photos of a rebellion in the possession of his brother (and assistant) Ignaty and ordered them both out of Moscow – despite the fact that Alexander Yagelsky was well-known to the Tsar and before long would be working exclusively for the imperial family. He travelled everywhere with them in later years, as familiar a part of their entourage as the doctor or the ladies-in-waiting, and he taught the imperial children to use cameras. But no exception was made for him: such was the importance that attached to photography.

The official images captured by Levitsky and Bergamasco, Pasetti, Hahn and others, come down to us as a window on a lost world. Through them we see the imperial family as their subjects and contemporaries saw them, in formal and less formal poses. But in recent years a second window has opened in the shape of their private albums: photographs taken by the family themselves or by members of their entourage and royal cousins. These were never intended for public view. Maria Feodorovna, the last

The photographic session must have been a tedious business, especially for the youngest members of the family. These portraits by Boissonas & Eggler of Grand Prince Alexander Mikhailovich, Grand Princess Ksenia Alexandrovna, their daughter Irina and youngest son Vasili, with Ksenia's sister Olga, come from a collection of at least twenty exposures, probably more, that were taken at the same sitting in about 1909. The sitting also involved the couple's five elder sons and various members of their household.

Tsar's mother, was the first keen amateur photographer in the imperial family and she seems to have acquired a camera in the late 1880s. By the 1890s it was not uncommon for snapshots taken at larger gatherings to include three or four family members all clutching cameras.

Maria Feodorovna's work was exhibited and she is said to have been asked to contribute to *The Photographic Art of Royal Persons*, a collection by a Munich publisher. Not surprisingly, her children caught the bug: Nicholas II seems to have had his first camera in his coronation year, 1896, and his later enjoyment of photography in all its forms is well known. His sister Ksenia took and developed photographs of her family, and their youngest brother Mikhail was given a camera in childhood and went on to become an active chairman of the St Petersburg Photographic Society. It was Mikhail whose enthusiasm for the pioneering colour work of Sergei Prokudin-Gorskii ensured the photographer an audience at court – first with Maria Feodorovna at Gatchina and then, in the winter of 1909, in the Alexander Palace before the Tsar and Tsaritsa. The Tsar was so impressed with the carefully selected colour slides shown to him that evening that he put his own resources behind the photographer's dream of documenting the Russian empire and its people; the project was still under way when war and Revolution intervened.

But the family's interest in photography was not limited to Maria Feodorovna and her children. Most of the Grand Princes used cameras: Konstantin Konstantinovich, poet, soldier, dramatist and President of the Imperial Academy of Science, certainly did, and his camera exists to this day. There are amateur photographs of his cousin Peter Nikolaevich's children dating from the early 1900s, and Peter's son Roman had a camera which he carried throughout his service in the First World War; he even used it while he was a prisoner of the Bolsheviks.

More and more now these private photographs are being rediscovered and made available through books and exhibitions. Mademoiselle Röhmer would have been horrified – but for us, access to these images adds a more human dimension to our understanding of the imperial family – their moments of relaxation, the laughter, the milestones of family life; a touching reminder that these were, after all, just ordinary human beings who happened to be trapped on one of history's most glittering stages.

On Names and Dates

Until February 1918 Russia used the old-style Julian calendar, which was twelve days behind the rest of Europe in the nineteenth century, thirteen in the twentieth. Where possible in this book, both dates are given for events in Russia.

There are various ways of expressing the names and titles of the imperial family. I prefer to use the accurate translation 'Grand Prince/Princess', reserving 'Grand Duke' for the German title 'Grossherzog', but 'Grand Duke/Duchess' is more commonly used for the Russian family and appears in some of the quotations, as do alternative spellings of their Christian names.

1

The Last Tsar

For most people the word 'tsar' conjures up images of the last Tsar, Nicholas II, and his family; for some, this is where knowledge of the Russian imperial family begins and ends. Nicholas II came to the throne as a young man of twenty-six in the autumn of 1894. He married within weeks of his accession and all of his five children were born 'in the purple' [to a reigning tsar] – something that had not happened in Russia on such a scale since the seventeenth century. The camera loved them. They were an attractive family and a natural subject for the illustrated magazines that were the media phenomenon of their day. Curiosity about the family remained high: through the 1890s and early 1900s articles were written by journalists, artists, courtiers – indeed, by anyone who had come into contact with the Russian Court at first- or second-hand and had a story to tell. Nicholas and Alexandra and their children were set apart by that peculiar combination of beauty, wealth and destiny that was theirs by accident of birth; the tragedy of the revolutionary years and the mystery that surrounded their fate for decades ensured that interest in them would never fade.

One of the most familiar photographs of the last Tsar's family, from the series taken for the 1913 Tercentenary when Russia celebrated 300 years of Romanov rule: (*left to right*) Grand Princess Maria, the Tsaritsa (between Grand Princess Tatiana and the Tsesarevich Alexei), the Tsar, Grand Princesses Olga and Anastasia. For this important moment the family chose a consciously domestic image.

The story of the last Tsar really begins with another Nicholas, his uncle the Tsesarevich Nikolai (*left*), eldest son of Tsar Alexander II. The Tsesarevich was a gifted, attractive young man, trained in a liberal tradition by the finest tutors available in the expectation that he would one day succeed his father. If he had lived, he would have reigned as Tsar Nicholas II. He was also the first member of the imperial family whose interest in photography has been documented. In the early 1860s he was presented with photographs of Russian street traders and hawkers taken by William Carrick, a Scot who lived in St Petersburg. Nikolai was so delighted that he presented Carrick with a diamond ring. He had his own collection of cartes-de-visite too, and it was from them that he chose his future wife . . .

Her name was Dagmar, 'Minny' to her family, and she was the second daughter of King Christian IX of Denmark. Nikolai acquired his first photograph of her in 1860, when he was seventeen and she twelve, and he came to love her from her photographs. His secretary, Feodor Oom, would later write of their first meeting, 'I recognised the young woman whose photograph the Grand Duke carried with him always and had often shown me.' This was at Fredensborg in Denmark in the summer of 1864. 'I came here as if in a fever,' Nikolai told his mother, 'I cannot tell you what came over me when we approached Fredensborg and I finally saw sweet Dagmar. How can I describe her? She is so pretty, direct, intelligent, lively yet at the same time shy. She is even prettier in real life than in the portraits that we had seen so far.' (*Right*) Nikolai with Dagmar's family at Fredensborg: (*left to right*) King Christian; Landgraf Wilhelm of Hesse-Cassel (her grandfather); Queen Louise in front of Dagmar; Nikolai; Princess Thyra of Denmark; Crown Prince Frederik in front of the Prince of Wales; Alexandra, Princess of Wales (Dagmar's sister); Valdemar (in front, their little brother); Marie, Princess Friedrich of Anhalt-Dessau (Queen Louise's sister) her daughter Princess Hilda of Anhalt-Dessau; Prince Julius of Glücksburg.

The engagement was announced in September 1864 but tragedy followed. Seven months later Nikolai died, and after the shock came the determination from both sets of parents that his brother Alexander, who was now forced into the position of Heir, should also inherit Dagmar. But Alexander was in love with his mother's maid-of-honour, Maria Elimovna Mestcherskaya. He tried to put her aside but could not face it, and in May 1866 he decided to renounce his right to the throne. 'I don't want any wife but M.E. It will be a radical transformation in my life, but with God's help, anything can be done . . .' This his father would not contemplate and after a furious argument Alexander was packed off to Denmark. In under two weeks his engagement to Dagmar was announced and this photograph, taken in June 1866, shows Dagmar and her family with her new fiancé: (*left to right*) Landgraf Wilhelm and Prince Julius; (*in front*) Grand Prince Vladimir; Princess Thyra, Dagmar and Alexander, Queen Louise, Prince Valdemar, King Christian and Crown Prince Frederik.

It should not have worked, but it did. Dagmar, who took the name 'Maria Feodorovna' on Orthodox baptism, and Alexander started their relationship with nothing in common but their grief for Nikolai: 'before I had even finished what I had to say, Minny threw her arms around my neck and started crying. I, too, could naturally not hold back tears . . . We talked and reminisced a great deal about Nixa and our memories of him' – this is how Alexander described the moment of his proposal. He was profoundly ill at ease in the public role of heir to the throne and the couple faced many tensions in their early years together. But they came through it all, to enjoy a happy and successful marriage.

And the first son, when he arrived, could have no other name but Nikolai. His Imperial Highness the Grand Prince Nikolai Alexandrovich, better known to history as Nicholas II and seen here with his mother, was born in the Alexander Palace at Tsarskoe Selo on 6/18 May 1868.

Nicholas in 1870. He was considered frail in infancy and would never share the impressive stature and bearing of the other Romanov princes, many of whom were well over six foot tall. There was also a sadness about him as a small child, which may have had something to do with the separations he endured in his earliest years when duty forced his parents away on tour. The summer of 1869 took them to the Caucasus, leaving Nicholas and his baby brother Alexander at home in the nursery. When they left again for the Caucasus the following spring, just two weeks after baby Alexander's death, Nicholas clung to his mother and was inconsolable.

Maria Feodorovna and Nicholas in 1871. The Tsarevna was a good mother who adored her children but she was inclined to possessiveness: she wanted them to remain young and dependant for as long as possible. This was characteristic of her family, and her sisters did the same; it guaranteed their offspring happiness in childhood, but did not always help them make the transition into adult life.

Nicholas (*centre*) with his mother and younger brother 'George', Grand Prince Georgi Alexandrovich, in about 1874/5. Georgi was born in the Alexander Palace, in the same room as his brother, on 27 April/9 May 1871. He appeared robust at first, but proved physically delicate and his health was a constant anxiety. He and Nicholas were close from childhood. It was in the spring of 1875 that their father's cousin Grand Prince Alexander Mikhailovich (a boy hardly older than they were) met them for the first time at Livadia in the Crimea. He would later recall Nicholas at that meeting as a 'cheerful boy in a little pink shirt, who stood on the marble steps of the long stairs in Livadia pointing at the sailing ships on the horizon and squinting his dreamy, curiously shaped eyes at the sunset . . .'.

By 1884 the family was complete. Grand Princess Ksenia (*centre*) was born in the spring of 1875 and Grand Prince Mikhail (*right*) in 1878, both in the Anichkov Palace in St Petersburg. In March 1881 their father succeeded to the throne, becoming Tsar Alexander III, and the youngest child, Olga, seen here in her mother's arms, made her appearance at Alexandria Peterhof in June 1882.

On Sunday 6/18 May 1884 the entire Russian empire celebrated Nicholas's sixteenth birthday and legal coming-of-age, when he swore the Oath of Allegiance in the Winter Palace in the presence of his family and representatives of the government, the church and the army. This had been an important rite of passage for all Romanov princes since the reign of Nicholas I. 'He looked very young and small to be the principal personage in such a ceremony,' *The Graphic* reported, 'but he has a bright, intelligent face, and is very like his mother. . . . In the church he boldly walked up alone to the altar, and, holding up his right hand over the bejewelled Bible and golden cross, repeated audibly and firmly, after the priest, the form of the oath. . . . After this the military formula of allegiance took place in the Throne Room. . . . St Petersburg was gaily decorated, and all night illuminated. There were also improvised theatres, popular games, and a flower show. Later, a sudden storm of wind and rain drove the sight-seers indoors.'

A few weeks later Nicholas would meet his future wife, Princess Alix of Hesse. They were second cousins and she was also one of his father's many godchildren, but the event that brought her to Russia was the wedding of her elder sister Elisabeth (*right*) to his uncle, Grand Prince Sergei Alexandrovich, in June. The girls' father, Grand Duke Ludwig IV, travelled north with his daughters and son for the event; his wife, Queen Victoria's daughter Princess Alice, had died of diphtheria in 1878. Imperial weddings involved days of celebration: in between, before and after, the families relaxed together at Peterhof on the coast, and Nicholas developed a childish attachment to Alix. He noted in his diary, 'Alix and I wrote our names on the rear window of the Italian house (we love each other). . . . Alix and Ernie [her brother] came to see us. We jumped about together on the net. Ernie, Alix and I told each other secrets. We had a terrific romp around the rooms of the Italian House. We all had dinner together, I sat and chatted to darling little Alix. Wrestled with Ernie.'

Ernst Ludwig (Ernie), Alix and Irene of Hesse in 1884. 'Alix' was not a nickname or diminutive like Ernie, but was the Princess's given name, chosen by Princess Alice at her daughter's birth in 1872 to avoid the constant mispronunciation her own name suffered in Germany: 'They murder my name here,' she told her mother, 'Aliicé' they pronounce it, so we thought 'Alix' could not so easily be spoilt.'

The Tsesarevich Nicholas in about 1887/8. He was an open-hearted, sociable young man who enjoyed the life of his regiment and the company of his cousins and childhood friends, the 'potatoes'. They gave themselves this nickname after a game of hare-and-hounds in the palace park at Gatchina. The 'hounds' lost the track and asked a peasant which way their friends had gone. The answer, 'They turned into potatoes' – meaning 'they turned into the potato field' – caused endless amusement and gave them their name. (The joke really only works in Russian, which has no definite or indefinite article.)

Grand Duke Ludwig in about 1889 with his daughters Alix (*left*) and Elisabeth, now Grand Princess Elizaveta Feodorovna but always known by her childhood diminutive 'Ella'. Alix visited her in Russia in January 1889 with their father and brother for the St Petersburg winter season. Elizaveta was not the only one to notice that the Tsesarevich was attracted to her sister and she did her utmost to encourage him. When her family left for Germany she gave him a framed photograph of Ernst Ludwig and Alix, with reminders painted around it of the things they had done together: 'the ice, the big hall, the skates, a clown, <u>the</u> window with 3 lights, a cotillon-ribbon and a basket with flowers from Aunt Sacha Narychkine's ball, the badminton articles, a branch of pink flowers. . . .' That summer Nicholas told his father that he hoped one day to marry Alix.

Princess Alix, taken during the 1889 visit. She saw Russia again with her father and elder sister Victoria in the summer of 1890; this time they stayed with Elizaveta and Sergei at Ilinskoe, a country house on the Moscow river which Sergei had inherited from his mother. For Alix the 1890 visit provided an unforgettable experience of a Russia far removed from the fashionable sophistication of the city. But the Tsesarevich, busy with regimental duties in and around St Petersburg, was not allowed to join her, much to his disappointment. In October he left Russia on the first stage of a tour of the Far East which would last for several months.

Nicholas remained faithful to the idea of marrying Princess Alix. But he was young and the world was full of attractions. He first met the ballerina Kshessinskaya (*right*) in June 1890 at the little theatre in the military encampment at Krasnoe Selo, where army manoeuvres were held each summer. In 1892 he began to visit her home with his cousins and a romantic attachment blossomed. He seemed intrigued by his own feelings: 'I've noticed something very strange within myself,' he noted in his diary on 1 April 1892. 'I never thought that two identical feelings, two loves could co-exist within the heart. I have loved Alix H for three years already and constantly cherish the hope that, God willing, one day I will marry her! . . . And since the summer camp of 1890 I have been passionately in love (platonically) with little K. The heart is a surprising thing!'

Princess Hélène of Orleans (*left*), whom Maria Feodorovna favoured as a potential bride for her son. There seems to be no real evidence that the Tsar and Tsaritsa were opposed to their son's choice of Alix, and suggestions that they were may be no more than gossip based on later events. Nicholas was allowed to make his feelings known to Alix more than once, but her constant refusals on religious grounds – she would not agree to convert to Orthodoxy – must have worried them. The Tsaritsa certainly looked elsewhere: 'While I was talking to Mama this morning,' Nicholas wrote on 29 January 1892, 'she made several hints about Helene, the daughter of the Comte de Paris, which puts me in an awkward position. I am at the crossing of two paths; I myself want to go in the other direction, while Mama obviously wants me to take this one! What will happen?' In 1895 Hélène married the Duke of Aosta at Kingston in Surrey.

The Tsesarevich, meanwhile, finally achieved his dream on the morning of 20 April 1894, in the Ehrenburg Palace in Coburg. Princess Alix, under pressure from various members of their two families, gave way and agreed to marry him. It was the outcome she too had wanted and years later she would look back on the day with pleasure, recalling every tiny detail. Whatever misgivings his mother may have had, she too was delighted on the day, and wrote to Nicholas from Russia, 'I was <u>so</u> happy and shed tears of <u>joy</u> and <u>emotion</u> and ran to announce this happy news to Papa first of all . . . and there were nothing but shouts of joy and real jubilation. . . . I hope dearest Alix will look upon me as a loving mother who'll receive her with open arms like her own dear child.'

The families had come together in Coburg for the wedding of Alix's brother to Victoria Melita of Edinburgh and Saxe-Coburg, who was a first cousin to both Alix and Nicholas. On 22 April, after the wedding celebrations, Nicholas left for Darmstadt with Alix and her family and it was in Darmstadt that this photograph was taken, in the garden of the Neues Palais, showing the two young couples: Ernst Ludwig and Victoria Melita, Grand Duke and Grand Duchess of Hesse, are on the right.

Alexander III was unwell from the start of 1894, but there was no great concern until the summer, when the doctors diagnosed kidney disease and prescribed a holiday in a drier climate. He died in the Crimea that autumn. Nicholas felt desolate and wholly unprepared. Princess Alix had been sent for shortly before the Tsar's death and converted to Orthodoxy in the private chapel at Livadia, taking the name 'Alexandra Feodorovna'. On 14/26 November 1894, shortly after the funeral, she and Nicholas were married in the Great Chapel of the Winter Palace. But the early days were not easy. On a personal level, Nicholas was still very much under the influence of his mother (*seen here with him, right*) and in Russia the elder Tsaritsa always had precedence. Maria Feodorovna was shattered by her husband's death and without him her eldest son became all the more important to her. However sincere her promise to be 'a loving mother' to his wife as well, she and Alexandra turned out to have little in common except the man whom each in her own way loved and needed. To make matters worse, for the first months of their married life the young Tsar and Tsaritsa lived under Maria Feodorovna's roof.

The young Tsaritsa in the early days of her marriage. By accident of fate Alexandra was forced to adapt to a new country with its own language, customs and beliefs, to married life and to the position of Empress all at once, and she was a reserved, serious young woman who took her responsibilities to heart. Within a few months pregnancy was added to the list . . .

Grand Princess Olga Nikolaevna was born in the Alexander Palace at Tsarskoe Selo at 9 o'clock on the evening of 3/15 November 1895, to the absolute delight of her parents. It was a difficult delivery: Alexandra was in labour for seven hours, supported through the ordeal by her mother-in-law, her sister Elizaveta and Nicholas. The summer of 1897 saw the arrival of a second daughter, Tatiana. A few months later, on the anniversary of his father's death, Nicholas told his mother, 'Our little daughters are growing, and turning into delightful happy little girls. Alix apologises deeply for not having sent you the photographs she promised, but you will at last receive them with this letter. Olga talks the same in Russian and in English and adores her little sister. Tatiana seems to us, understandably, a very beautiful child, her eyes have become dark and large. She is <u>always</u> happy and only cries once a day without fail, after her bath when they feed her.'

The imperial family was overwhelmingly a family of boys. Each individual family unit within the dynasty had more sons than daughters in a pattern stretching back over decades, and to a Tsar a son was all-important. The Family Statutes laid down by Tsar Paul, Nicholas's great-great-grandfather, at the beginning of the century made it impossible for a girl to inherit the throne while the male line of the dynasty endured. On 2/24 June 1899 Alexandra produced a third daughter, Maria (*left, with her mother and centre, above and below*). Privately the family were as delighted as any family would be with the birth of a beautiful, healthy child. 'She was born good, I often think,' her nurse wrote, 'with the very smallest trace of original sin possible.' But on the streets the celebrations were wearing thin. People expected a Tsesarevich.

After the birth of the fourth daughter, Anastasia (*left, with her mother*), in the early summer of 1901, even close family could hardly contain their feelings: 'My God! What a disappointment! . . . a fourth girl!' wrote Nicholas's sister Ksenia in her diary, and their cousin Grand Prince Konstantin Konstantinovich remarked, 'Forgive us, Lord, if we all felt disappointment instead of joy; we were so hoping for a boy and it's a fourth daughter.' The pressure on Alexandra was intense.

The Tsar proudly holding their son, His Imperial Highness the Grand Prince Tsesarevich Alexei Nikolaevich, born in the Alexandria Dacha at Peterhof at a quarter past one on 30 July/12 August 1904. It was a difficult time for Russia – the country was at war with Japan but the birth of an heir was an event that had been despaired of and the celebration throughout the empire was intense. One of Alexandra's maids-of-honour, Sophie Buxhoeveden, described the scene in a small village church near Kazan as the birth was proclaimed: 'every man, woman and child had squeezed in to listen to the imperial message. The deacon . . . wore the holiday cloth of silver vestments, much too large for him . . . He cleared his throat, spat discreetly behind his hand . . . and slowly boomed out: "We, Nicholas II, by the Grace of God Emperor of Russia, Tsar of Muscovy." All the imperial titles were rolled out in a crescendo. The men, mostly old soldiers, stood rigidly at attention . . . The women crossed themselves, and bowed low as every title of the Emperor was mentioned . . .'

(*Right*) Alexei was surrounded by an aura of gratitude and delight. On Sophie Buxhoeveden's first visit to the Alexander Palace she was invited into Alexandra's private sitting-room where the four little Princesses were playing, 'all dressed alike in white, low-necked frocks of embroidered cambric with blue bows in their hair [they] greeted me shyly, looking at me curiously as if I were some new species of wild animal.' Three-year-old Anastasia made the first move and very quickly Sophie was drawn into a game of blind man's buff: 'Little Marie, aged six, pulled at my belt. Turning quickly in the unfamiliar room, I should have collapsed into an armchair had not the Empress's laughing voice warned me. "Stop! Danger! Turn to the left." I finally caught the ten-year-old . . . Olga, when our game came to an end. "Stop, all of you," said the Empress. "Baby's coming." I unbound my eyes, and saw the nurse come in, carrying the three-month-old Cesarevich. He was a splendid baby . . . two delightful dimples appeared in his cheeks as he crowed and stretched out his arms towards his mother. I shall never forget the look on the Empress's face as she took him from the nurse . . .'

The imperial children in 1906. (*Left to right*): Alexei, Olga, Tatiana, Maria, Anastasia.

(*Left*) Alexandra and her children on her balcony at the Alexander Palace – a favourite place for sitting outside in good weather and the site of many well-known photographs.

(*Facing page*) Grand Princesses Olga (*top left*), Tatiana (*top right*), Maria (*bottom left*) and Anastasia (*bottom right*), from a series of official portraits taken on 21 May/3 June 1914.

(*Below*) The imperial children in 1910.

The four imperial daughters were rarely far from one another. 'It would have been difficult to find four sisters with characters more dissimilar and yet so perfectly blended in an affection which did not exclude personal independence, and, in spite of contrasting temperaments, kept them a most united family. . . The eldest, Olga Nicolaevna, possessed a remarkably quick brain. She had good reasoning powers as well as initiative, a very independent manner, and a gift for swift and entertaining repartee. . . . Tatiana Nicolaevna was rather reserved, essentially well balanced, and had a will of her own, though she was less frank and spontaneous than her elder sister. She was not so gifted, either, but this inferiority was compensated by more perseverance and balance. . . . Marie Nicolaevna was a fine girl, tall for her age, and a picture of glowing health and colour. She had large and beautiful grey eyes. Her tastes were very simple, and with her warm heart she was kindness itself. . . . Anastasie Nicolaevna, on the other hand, was very roguish and almost a wag. She had a very strong sense of humour, and the darts of her wit often found sensitive spots. . . . She was so lively, and her gaiety so infectious . . .'

Nicholas, Alexandra and Alexei. The Tsar's ADC Colonel Mordvinov said of Alexei: 'He had what we Russians usually call "a golden heart". He easily felt an attachment to people, he liked them and tried to do his best to help them, especially when it seemed to him that someone was unjustly hurt. His love, like that of his parents, was based mainly on pity. Tsesarevich Alexei Nikolaevich was an awfully lazy, but very capable boy (I think, he was lazy precisely because he was capable), he easily grasped everything, he was thoughtful and keen beyond his years. . . . Despite his good nature and compassion, he undoubtedly promised to possess a firm and independent character in the future.'

2

The Family

Nicholas II grew up in a large extended family of uncles, aunts and cousins and, though he had friends among the aristocracy, these were the people with whom most of his time was spent and the people he could naturally have expected to turn to for companionship, understanding and practical support. The family into which he was born divided into four distinct branches, descending from the four sons of his great-grandfather Nicholas I: Alexander II, Konstantin, Nikolai and Mikhail. Then there were other cousins, of Leuchtenberg, Oldenburg and Mecklenburg-Strelitz, tracing their lineage back either to Nicholas I or to his father Tsar Paul. They were, for the most part, a lively, intelligent, disparate group of people bound together by a genuine love of their country and by the knowledge that the Tsar's interest was their interest. Nicholas I instituted the Oath of Allegiance which bound the branches of the dynasty to the main tree. Alexander II combined this with a more informal approach, holding regular family meals which all adult members of the family were expected to attend and going out of his way to befriend the next generation. It was Alexander III who broke ranks for the first time by making it plain that there were members of the family he did not trust; still, he continued to hold family meals and other gatherings. Apartments were reserved for all the cousins in his main residence at Gatchina. It was only after his death that the family began to divide.

A famous photograph taken by Sergei Levitsky in about 1870, which places the last Tsar firmly in the context of the wider family. Nicholas is the baby in the centre on his mother's knee, with his father Alexander standing behind. The others (*from the left*) are his young uncles, Grand Princes Pavel and Sergei, their father Alexander II and his other children: Grand Princess Maria, Grand Prince Alexei and (*on the right*) Grand Prince Vladimir, leaning on the chair of their mother, Tsaritsa Maria Alexandrovna. But the photo is not all it seems: it is, in fact, a splendid example of how the camera, even in those very early days, could be made to lie. In another version of the same picture, Grand Prince Vladimir leans on an empty chair. The figure of the Tsaritsa has been added – skilfully, but no skill could hide the fact that the light is falling on her face from the right hand side while every other figure in the group is lit from the left. The earlier version of the photograph also has a plain curtain for a background, so the setting here has been painted in – and it is even possible that the whole picture is a composite of several individual or smaller group portraits.

The early Verry cartes of Alexander II and Maria Alexandrovna which date from about 1856. The pose with one hand up to the chin seems to have been characteristic of Maria Alexandrovna; she adopts it in many of her portraits.

An early, unattributed set of cartes-de-visite of the children of Alexander II from the Grand-Ducal family archives in Darmstadt (home of their mother's family). They date from about 1859 and show (*left*) the Tsesarevich Nikolai, whose tragically early death robbed Russia of a promising Tsar and his brother Alexander of the chance to escape the Court life he hated; (*below left*) Alexander Alexandrovich himself, the future Tsar Alexander III; (*below*) Vladimir Alexandrovich, Alexander's rival and sparring partner who was said to have nursed ambition from an early age, based on the knowledge that his grandfather Nicholas I was a third son like himself.

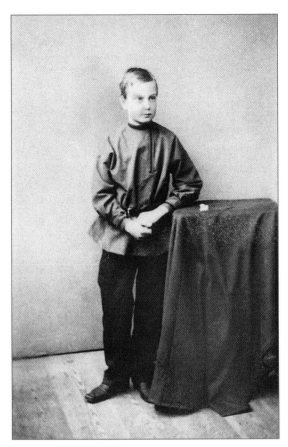

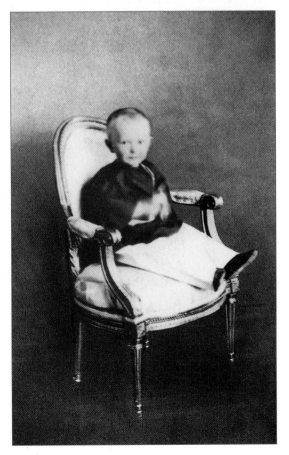

Alexei Alexandrovich (*above left*), who was
destined for service in the Russian navy from
early childhood. A German cousin remembered
him at their first meeting in 1857: 'a boy in a
white suit who was very lively, and who used to
tease me. I envied him frightfully because he was
seven years old and did not have to be brought
in, but was allowed to sit at table with his elders';
(*above right*) Maria Alexandrovna, who occupied
a special place in the affections of both her
parents as the only surviving girl in the family
(their eldest child, also a girl, had died in 1849,
shortly before her seventh birthday); and (*right*)
Sergei Alexandrovich, born in 1857.

Alexander II with his infant son, Grand Prince Pavel, who was born in 1860. The Tsar and his brothers were far more involved in the business of childbirth, infancy and the nursery than British men of their class and generation would have dreamed of being. They supported their wives through each birth as a matter of course and exchanged intimate details of the process of the delivery and of the physical health of mother and baby in the weeks that followed. It was after Pavel's birth that the Tsaritsa Maria Alexandrovna's health showed signs of serious decline (she had tuberculosis). He was her last child.

Alexander III as a boy (*right*), as Tsesarevich (*below left*) and as Tsar, at Livadia with his family in about 1893: (*left to right*) Nicholas, Georgi, Maria Feodorovna, Olga, Mikhail, Ksenia and the Tsar. Alexander was an interesting character. Large and awkward in boyhood, and always considered boorish and uncivilised, he possessed unexpected touches of delicacy and refinement. He commissioned the first Fabergé egg, for example, and kept a collection of miniature animals made of glass and china for his own amusement, which he sometimes showed to his children. The extracts of his diary that have so far been published – and he kept a diary from 1861, when he was sixteen, until 1881, the year of his accession – show great emotion and the gift for self-expression that he was said to have lacked in person. His elder brother's death threw him into a position he had never wanted and did not feel suited to, and he reacted in the early years with unpredictable fits of temper. It was hard for him to master his own nature and adapt: his success was a considerable achievement.

If Alexander had failed, the next brother Grand Prince Vladimir Alexandrovich, seen here in about 1861, would have been called to fill the breach. A few weeks after her husband's accession, their mother told one of her ladies about a curious conversation she had had with her sons. She heard Nikolai, the eldest, say to Vladimir, who was then just five years old, 'When you are Tsar . . .'. She interrupted, reminding him that his brother was never likely to inherit the throne, but Nikolai was adamant: 'No, he will, his name means "ruler of the world" . . . Grandfather was a third son, and he became Tsar. I will die, then Sasha will be Tsar. But Sasha will die too, then Vladimir will take over.' This story was put in writing when the brothers were still children and no one could guess what would happen to them, but it foreshadowed later events. If Alexander had renounced his rights as he wanted, Vladimir would indeed have taken over. The knowledge that he had come so close would never leave Vladimir: in later years his attitude to his nephew Nicholas as Tsar was both patronising and dictatorial.

The three youngest children (*from the left*) Pavel, Maria and Sergei, seen here in about 1863, formed a close-knit group within the family. As small children they spent long periods outside Russia with their mother, when ill-health forced her to travel. She clung to them – all the more so because she had been devoted to Nikolai and after his death felt that she had neglected her other children for him. Pavel was everyone's favourite: 'My little Puss-in-Boots', she called him.

In the 1850s and 1860s Alexander II had five surviving siblings: two sisters and three brothers. The eldest was Grand Princess Maria Nikolaevna (*right*), who is said to have refused to marry unless she could remain in Russia. Consequently her children grew up alongside her brothers' families and they remained close. Her first husband, Maximilian, 3rd Duke of Leuchtenberg, fitted into the definition of suitable marriage partners laid down by Tsar Paul, though it was not a grand match. Her father made him an 'Imperial Highness' and as a couple they played a very full part in the life of the country, contributing to artistic and charitable causes. They had seven children and the Duke died in 1852. In 1854 Maria is said to have married for a second time, in secret, to Count Grigori Stroganov; officially the marriage did not take place until 1856, after her father's death. It was an act he would never have approved. 'No doubt she was a hundred times more worthy than I was,' her sister Olga wrote, 'she was more talented than the seven of us put together and there was only one thing she lacked: a sense of duty.'

Olga Nikolaevna herself, the second sister, as Queen of Württemberg. She was a beautiful, gentle girl who lacked the impulsiveness of her elder sister and was content to leave her future in her father's hands – though his determination to secure a prestigious match for her almost saw her end without any husband, though there was no shortage of interested young men. In the summer of 1846 the Tsar finally agreed her marriage to Karl, Hereditary Prince of Württemberg. It is usually said that this was an unhappy marriage though, in a memoir of her early years written for the children she regarded as her granddaughters, her great-nieces Olga and Elsa of Württemberg, Queen Olga wrote fondly of her engagement and wedding. Childlessness was her great sorrow; the nearest she would know to a child of her own was her niece, Grand Princess Vera Konstantinovna, who spent long periods with her and married into the Württemberg family. Queen Olga spent over four decades of her life in Germany and always craved contact with her own, Russian family.

Grand Prince Konstantin Nikolaevich (*left*), second son of Nicholas I, who was destined from childhood for a career in the navy and was educated and trained by the distinguished sailor, geographer, Arctic explorer and President of the Academy of Science, Feodor Litke. At eight years old he was given command of the warship *Hercules* – presumably in name only – and at seventeen he took active command of the brig *Ulysses*, sailing in the Gulf of Finland. Konstantin was academically gifted – as an adult he built up an important library, principally on scientific and nautical subjects, though he collected contemporary literature too; he was also musical and artistic. Politically, he was more determined on liberal reform than his elder brother – or simply less daunted by its problems. He was a strong man in every sense, but one given to intolerance and temper; always fond of his nephew the Tsesarevich Nikolai, he never hid his dislike of Grand Prince Alexander and this, in the end, would be his downfall.

The elder 'Konstantinovichi', as they were known in the family: Grand Prince Konstantin's children (*left to right*) Grand Princess Vera, Grand Princes Nikolai and Konstantin and Grand Princess Olga, in about 1860. The family was completed with the birth of two younger sons, Dmitri and Viacheslav, in 1860 and 1862.

Grand Princess Alexandra Petrovna, wife of Nicholas I's third son Grand Prince Nikolai, with their elder son, also named Nikolai and distinguished as 'Nikolai Nikolaevich the younger', again in about 1860. A second son, Piotr (Peter), was born in 1864. Together the brothers were the first generation of the 'Nikolaevichi'.

Grand Prince Nikolai Nikolaevich the elder (*above*) was a soldier for most of his life, first seeing active service in the Crimean War when he was in his early twenties. His rapid rise through the ranks of command owed a great deal to who he was, but much also to natural ability. He enjoyed army life and hunting; he took great interest in all aspects of the management of his estates, but he does not seem to have been a man who inspired great affection, even in those closest to him.

His younger brother Grand Prince Mikhail, on the other hand (*right*), kept the respect and love of the family through three generations, eventually becoming its elder statesman and a man trusted implicitly by three Tsars in turn – four, if we include his father. Like his brother Nikolai, he too was a soldier and first saw action in the Crimea. He is seen here with his wife, Grand Princess Olga Feodorovna, and their two elder children, Nikolai and Anastasia, in about 1862. The 'Mikhailovichi' were the most numerous of the three junior branches of the family and there were to be five more children, all boys: Mikhail, Georgi, Alexander, Sergei and Alexei.

Tsaritsa Maria Alexandrovna with her youngest sons, Sergei and Pavel, in about 1867.

(*Above left*) Alexander II with Milord. In 1867 the Tsar and Tsaritsa still shared concerns about his work, their children and the wider family. Affection and understanding would always exist between them, but Alexander's passions had moved on. Maria Alexandrovna was a sick woman, obliged to spend long periods abroad. In the early 1860s the Tsar made a visit on her behalf to the prestigious Smolny Institute, a school for well-born young women. One pupil caught his eye. Princess Ekaterina Dolgorukaya (*above, in Smolny uniform and right, in the late 1870s*) was an imperial ward, about fifteen years old and very homesick. The Tsar's visits increased. In 1865 Ekaterina left the Smolny early. Alexander asked her to be his mistress; she refused him for a year, then gave way, and for the next fourteen years they enjoyed an intensely passionate relationship. She lived in a series of houses in the city, seeing few other people; he made afternoon visits. For form's sake their children – there were four, one of whom died in infancy – lived in a separate house. It was a 'secret' the whole world knew. In the weeks following the Tsaritsa's death in 1880 Alexander fulfilled a long-standing promise and married his 'Katya', creating the title Prince/Princess Yurievsky for her and the children.

By the early 1890s the grandsons of Nicholas I were almost all grown men and a new generation was well on its way to adulthood. This group, taken in 1892 at the military settlement of Krasnoe Selo, shows representatives of three generations gathered for the summer manoeuvres. (*Front row, seated*) Grand Princess Ksenia (Alexander III's daughter), Maria Pavlovna (wife of Grand Prince Vladimir), her daughter Elena Vladimirovna, Grand Princess Alexandra Iosifovna (widow of Grand Prince Konstantin Nikolaevich), Tsaritsa Maria Feodorovna, Alexander III, Grand Princes Mikhail Nikolaevich (the Tsar's youngest uncle) and Pavel Alexandrovich (the Tsar's youngest brother). (*Immediately behind*) Dukes Carl-Michael and Georg of Mecklenburg Strelitz (great-grandsons of Tsar Paul), Grand Prince Konstantin Konstantinovich, his sister Grand Princess Olga, Queen of the Hellenes, Tsesarevich Nicholas (later Nicholas II), Grand Princes Vladimir Alexandrovich and Dmitri Konstantinovich (in the white hat), Duke Peter of Oldenburg (a great-great-grandson of Tsar Paul on his father's side, and on his mother's a great-grandson of Nicholas I) and Duke Georgi of Leuchtenberg (a great-grandson of Nicholas I). (*Back row*) Grand Princes Sergei Mikhailovich and Nikolai Nikolaevich the younger, Duke Alexander of Oldenburg (Duke Peter's father, peering over the shoulder of Grand Prince Dmitri). The boys in front are Alexei Mikhailovich, the youngest of the Mikhailovichi, who died of tuberculosis at the age of nineteen, Mikhail Alexandrovich (Alexander III's son) and brothers Andrei and Boris Vladimirovich (Grand Prince Vladimir's sons).

(*Facing page*) The Konstantinovichi in the early 1900s: (*above*) Grand Princesses Olga, Queen of the Hellenes (*right*), and her sister Vera, Duchess Wilhelm Eugen of Württemberg; (*below*) their younger brothers, Grand Princes Konstantin (*left*) and Dmitri. By this time the youngest brother, Viacheslav, was dead, while the elder, Nikolai, had been officially removed from the lists of the imperial family following a series of scandals (*see page 105*).

(*Above, left and right*) Grand Princes Nikolai and Peter Nikolaevich. Every man in the imperial family held military rank but for Nikolai Nikolaevich the younger, the army was a way of life and an abiding interest. His other passion was hunting. Chronic lung disease forced his brother to spend much of his time in the benign climate of the Crimea and Peter's mind turned to more peaceful pursuits, particularly architecture. He was a profoundly loyal man: first to his brother, then to the Tsar.

(*Left*) Grand Prince Nikolai Mikhailovich, who published several history books based on his researches in the family archives. An ardent Francophile, he became an elected member of the Académie Française: his love of France influenced his politics too, and he veered towards what he called 'authoritarian republicanism'. Nikolai's political ambitions became apparent during the Revolution. He was a vehement critic of most of his male cousins and a divisive influence among them.

(*Above left*) Grand Princess Anastasia Mikhailovna, Grand Duchess of Mecklenburg-Schwerin.

(*Above right*) Grand Prince Mikhail Mikhailovich with his wife Sophie, Countess Torby, in what appears to be a formal portrait in Court dress. In fact, the couple were never able to appear at Court as Mikhail was banished from Russia by Alexander III for contracting his marriage without permission, and contrary to the family laws.

(*Right*) Grand Prince Georgi Mikhailovich with his daughters Ksenia (*centre*) and Nina. A close friend of Grand Prince Peter, Georgi Mikhailovich was less assertive than his brothers and more willing to fit in as a member of the dynasty. After a leg injury made active military service impossible he became director of the Alexander III Museum, established by Nicholas II in one of the family's former palaces in St Petersburg (and still in existence as the Russian Museum). Georgi was a knowledgeable and highly respected coin collector and wrote several monographs on the subject.

(*Above*) Grand Prince Alexander Mikhailovich, his wife Grand Princess Ksenia Alexandrovna (Alexander III's daughter) and their children, (*left to right*) Prince Rostislav, Grand Prince Alexander, Grand Princess Ksenia holding the hand of her youngest son, Prince Vasili, Prince Nikita (sitting in front), Princess Irina, Prince Feodor, Prince Dmitri, Prince Andrei. Initially very close to Nicholas II and his wife, Alexander Mikhailovich was too fiercely critical of the other Grand Princes and of the workings of the imperial government and Court to remain comfortable among them for long. From 1906 he and his family spent long periods out of Russia, living in the south of France.

(*Left*) Grand Prince Sergei Mikhailovich. An artilleryman who rose to the position of Inspector General of the Russian Artillery, Sergei Mikhailovich was one of Nicholas II's closest friends when they were young and, according to his brother Alexander, he also loved Nicholas's sister Ksenia before she accepted Alexander's proposal. His sister-in-law Marie, wife of his brother Georgi Mikhailovich, remembered him as 'one of my best friends in Russia. . . . His sense of the ridiculous was extremely keen, and many a time [we] got into trouble because of our love of laughter.' A pessimist with a dark sense of humour, Sergei never married but remained the friend and protector – perhaps also the lover – of the dancer Mathilde Kschessinskaya.

3

Marrying into the Family

One of the most successful sovereigns of the Romanov dynasty was Catherine the Great, who reigned from 1762 to 1796. So profound a stamp did she put on her country's history that it would be all too easy to forget that Russia was not really her country at all. She crossed the border as a girl of fifteen, when her name was Sophia, Princess of Anhalt-Zerbst and her nationality German. In the generations that followed, almost every bride accepted into the imperial family came from abroad: the duty placed on Romanov men to choose a partner of royal birth made this inevitable. Year on year they came, uprooted from family, language, culture and religious practice and forced to learn these things anew, while also adapting to married life. Even their names were left behind. The transition was never easy; for some it could be a nightmare. Cultural barriers became more pronounced as the nineteenth century lasted: in Nicholas I's family, for example, the parents and elder children spoke French as their first language while the younger sons spoke Russian. This increasing sense of national identity made the pressure to assimilate ever more strong. Yet the Romanov brides proved to be a resourceful group of women, contributing in their own distinctive ways to the country of their adoption and bringing their own influences to bear on the family.

Two representatives of the earliest generation we can reach through photographs: (*left*) Empress Alexandra Feodorovna, wife of Nicholas I and mother of Alexander II, who began life as Princess Charlotte of Prussia. She first met Grand Prince Nikolai Pavlovich, then only the younger brother of a Tsar, at her father's Court in Berlin when he was seventeen and she fifteen; she arrived in Russia in the summer of 1817, when she was eighteen years old, changed her name on Orthodox baptism and was married in the Great Chapel of the Winter Palace on her nineteenth birthday. She became Empress in 1825 when her husband succeeded his brother Alexander I. Alexandra Feodorovna belonged to a generation of women who were expected to do very little beyond looking decorative and bearing children and she did both to perfection. Her husband was attentive and adoring and she presided with natural grace over a Court where life was one long series of entertainments. Lady Londonderry visited Russia in 1837 and was told of the Empress 'that for the twenty years she has been in this country she has given so much happiness and she has never done harm to a soul'.

(*Right*) Alexandra's sister-in-law Grand Princess Elena Pavlovna, born Princess Charlotte of Württemberg. After an unconventional upbringing in post-Revolutionary Paris, Charlotte's future was settled by her family when she was fifteen. She had never met Grand Prince Mikhail Pavlovich, Alexander I's youngest brother. He had no interest in marriage. Nonetheless, a year after their engagement he received her at the border where she impressed everyone with her poise and intelligence. They married in February 1824 but it was a miserable business. Though Elena produced a succession of children, all of them girls, Mikhail treated her with callous indifference. Only his elder brother saw how desperate her situation was – 'one must agree that this young and charming woman was very gratuitously and very uselessly sacrificed. Her position is frightful.' Elena tried to leave Russia in 1827 but the imperial family would allow only a temporary separation. After that, though, her fortunes improved and the list of her achievements in Russia is formidable. The arts, music, medical charities and institutions all benefited from her patronage; she was also a moving force behind political change, encouraging her nephews Alexander II and Konstantin in the path of reform.

(*Right*) Maria Alexandrovna, Marie of Hesse-Darmstadt, was fourteen with the long, loose hair of childhood when she first met the future Alexander II. She was eating cherries when she was ushered forward and had to spit the stones into her hand before she could speak to him. 'This was Marie, our beloved Marie, who became Sasha's happiness,' his sister Olga remembered. 'From the first word she spoke his feelings were aroused. She was no doll like the others, there was no coyness about her and she expected nothing from their meeting.' The engagement was approved and they married three years later. Maria was intelligent and there was a profound seriousness about her. She could not make the necessary conversion to Orthodoxy without meaning it; without becoming, in the course of time, more devoutly Orthodox than many native Russians. She cared deeply about the country: she and Alexander always discussed his work and he respected her judgement. She also put her resources behind women's education and medicine. Maria Alexandrovna was greatly loved in the family, but she lacked the easy, social gifts that made other empresses popular.

(*Left*) Grand Princess Alexandra Iosifovna was a Saxe-Altenburg by birth and Nicholas I noticed her in 1846, her sixteenth year: by that autumn his second son Konstantin was in Altenburg. The effect of their first meeting was electrifying. 'I don't know what has happened to me,' eighteen-year-old Konstantin wrote, 'I am a completely different person. Only one thought moves me, I have only one picture before my eyes: always and only she, my angel, my star. I really believe I am in love. But how long have I known her? Just a few hours and already I'm up to my ears in love . . .' He sustained the excitement until their wedding on 30 August/11 September 1848, and for many years after. Alexandra was more at ease in society than Maria, less prone to homesickness. According to the lady-in-waiting Anna Tiutcheva, she was neither clever nor especially well-educated: 'she takes the place of a spoilt child in the family and they treat her frequent tactlessness and lapses in behaviour as jolly pranks.' But this was only in the early days: in time she would become a strong and respected figure within the dynasty.

Grand Princess Olga Feodorovna, Princess Cäcilie of Baden, was born at Karlsruhe in 1839. The story of her meeting with Grand Prince Mikhail Nikolaevich has not been recorded but the marriage was a love match and Cäcilie was lucky: of the four sons of Nicholas I, Mikhail alone remained faithful throughout married life. She was sixteen at the time of the engagement. Mikhail told his sister-in-law Maria Alexandrovna that he had chosen the name 'Olga Feodorovna' because he did not like 'Cäcilie'. They married in the Winter Palace on 16/28 August 1857: 'I have prayed fervently,' Mikhail wrote in his diary, 'and thanked God with all my heart that I was permitted to see this day.' As a couple, the 'Michels' were generally well liked; 'most amiable and friendly', Queen Victoria found them, and she thought the Grand Princess 'very good humoured, merry and agreeable'. Mikhail she thought, 'really quite charming – so mild and gentle. . . . We were charmed with him, and I hear wherever he goes – high and low, love him.' Her daughter called him 'a <u>creature of gold</u> in every respect'.

In 1862 Grand Prince Mikhail was appointed Viceroy of the Caucasus, a position he held for nearly twenty years. He and the Grand Princess held Court in the palace in Tiflis and four of their seven children were Caucasian-born – Olga Feodorovna is seen here with the fifth son, Sergei. Despite living so far from the capital, she assimilated completely into the ways of her husband's country and thought of herself as entirely Russian. The position of Vicereine allowed her a degree of autonomy at her husband's side and she gave the Caucasus its first girls' schools and training institutes for women; she was also involved in medical work, particularly during the Russian–Turkish war of 1877–8. She liked to know what was happening around her and her observations could be telling. One of her ladies-in-waiting of later years described her as 'an unusually clever woman, with a sharp critical sense. In some circles she was rather dreaded for her malicious but striking and pertinent remarks. I personally experienced only kind attentions and consideration from her . . .'

Grand Princess Alexandra Iosifovna with her elder children in about 1863: Nikolai, the eldest, is behind his mother; the others are, from the left, Konstantin, Vera, Dmitri and Olga, and the photograph on the right shows the children's father. But by this time the unity expressed in the photograph was passing. In the mid-1860s the Grand Prince began a relationship with the dancer Anna Kousnetsova, fathering a second family.

Duchess Alexandra of Oldenburg (*left*) belonged to a German family but grew up in St Petersburg. Her father was a grandson of Tsar Paul. She married Grand Prince Nikolai Nikolaevich in 1856, becoming Grand Princess Alexandra Petrovna, and their first child was born before the year's end. Alexandra Petrovna was a gifted artist. She had no time for Court life and no interest in fine clothes – much to her husband's disgust. Medicine fascinated her: the Grand Prince provided her with a hospital and she devoted ever more time to its work. She founded a training institute for nurses in St Petersburg while he followed his elder brothers and found a mistress. This photograph from the 1870s shows her in nurse's uniform. In the late '70s she moved to Kiev, establishing a convent with its own hospital and clinic, to provide free treatment for the poor. She took orders as 'Sister Anastasia' and became abbess: today her grave in the convent garden is again tended by nuns and her work continues.

Maria Feodorovna with her children Mikhail and Ksenia, probably taken after her husband's accession in the spring of 1881. For decades the imperial family had been very German in character and sympathy, with close ties to the Prussian Court, but the coming of Maria Feodorovna, Princess Dagmar of Denmark, marked a change. Her first fiancé, the Tsesarevich Nikolai, was adamant that she was his own choice and the match had no political implications: nonetheless, Prussia and Denmark were at war shortly before the engagement and the antipathy between the two countries lasted for decades. The falling-away of Prussian sympathies at the Russian Court in the reign of Alexander III was due in part to his wife's influence. Despite her commitment to her husband's country, Maria Feodorovna remained very Danish and always did her best to promote Danish interests in Russia.

But German sympathies persisted at the Court of Alexander's brother Grand Prince Vladimir, seen here with his fiancée, Duchess Marie of Mecklenburg-Schwerin. Marie was a great-great-granddaughter of Tsar Paul. When she met Vladimir for the first time in 1871 she was seventeen years old and had just become engaged – by her own choice – to a much older German Prince; she broke off the engagement immediately, though it took almost three years to secure Vladimir. The attraction was mutual, the problem that Marie flatly refused to convert to Orthodoxy, a step that had been demanded of every Romanov bride for generations. For three years the negotiations continued; then, in the spring of 1874, Alexander II gave way and allowed the engagement to go ahead. It was not a popular decision in Russia, particularly with those princesses who had already converted. It marked the arrival of an assertive and self-confident young woman who would become a formidable force within the family.

Grand Princess Maria Pavlovna – Marie's married name – with her second son Grand Prince Kirill in about 1878. An elder son, Alexander, had died in 1877 when he was not quite two years old. Maria Pavlovna revelled in the splendour and wealth of St Petersburg and before long had become the centre of the fashionable set – all those who were not accepted in the more traditional environment of the Imperial Court gravitated naturally towards her. She liked being at the centre. A woman of immense charm, she was at her best when offering guidance to anyone younger or less experienced than herself. She would have made a magnificent empress but her nature rebelled against taking second place. She and her elder sister-in-law the Tsarevna, and later Empress, Maria Feodorovna (*opposite*), were rivals from the start.

Princess Elisabeth of Saxe-Altenburg was sixteen in the summer of 1882, when Konstantin Konstantinovich visited Altenburg. He was twenty-four and getting over a disappointed love, and the attraction between them was immediate. But while Elisabeth had no doubts, Konstantin agonised. He was a profoundly introspective man and a year passed in which he failed to write to Elisabeth as promised, though he wrote poems about her; then he returned to propose marriage. In April 1884 Elisabeth arrived in Russia. She had chosen to keep her Lutheran faith. This was hard for Konstantin to accept because his own devotion to Orthodoxy was profound. Worse still, Elisabeth offended the Court by refusing to kiss the cross held up in services. Konstantin's fears were aroused, but on the wedding morning she wrote to reassure him: 'I promise you, that I will never do anything to anger or hurt you through our divided religions. . . . I can only tell you again, <u>how very much</u> I love you.'

Konstantin's mind was eased, and he carried Elisabeth's letter in his pocket all that day. Of the Orthodox service itself, he wrote, 'After the words "God our Lord, by Glory and Honour marry this couple!" I saw Elisabeth already as my wife, who is given to me for ever and whom I should love, take care of and caress. The moment when the Priest led us to the altar-stand was especially solemn for me, I felt light and happy. . . . We were man and wife. We were permitted to kiss one another. Then we went to His Majesty, the Tsaritsa and my parents. The service began. The singing was wonderful. A stone had fallen from my heart . . .' Wedding photographs of the imperial family in the nineteenth century are rare, but this shows Elisabeth, Grand Princess Elizaveta Mavrikievna, on her wedding day, wearing the bridal crown – during the Orthodox wedding service crowns are held above the heads of the couple, usually by younger male relatives. Putting their awkward beginning behind them, Elisaveta and Konstantin settled happily together. He called her 'Lilinka'. A month after the wedding he told his father 'she belongs to us already'.

The Vladimirs: Grand Princess Maria Pavlovna and her husband and children in 1884. The children are, from left to right, Boris, Elena, Kirill and Andrei.

Elisabeth of Hesse wavered for more than a year before accepting Grand Prince Sergei Alexandrovich (*centre*), whom she had known from childhood. He too was hesitant but they became engaged in September 1883, and her father told Alexander III, 'I did not hesitate to consent because I have known Sergei since he was a child. I see his nice, pleasant manners and I am sure that he will make my daughter happy.' Private letters now coming to light make nonsense of the old idea that Elisabeth's marriage was one long martyrdom. That came largely from Court gossip and from the writings of Grand Prince Alexander Mikhailovich, who hated Sergei. A deeply religious man who made no secret of his contempt for fashionable society, Sergei did make enemies. 'He was often self-conscious,' Elisabeth's brother Ernst Ludwig (*right*) remembered. 'Then he stiffened and his eyes looked hard . . . from this people gained a false impression of him and thought him proud and cold, which he certainly was not. There were many, very many people he helped, but only in the strictest secrecy.' 'Sergei is a person,' Elisabeth told her father, 'of whom the more one is with him, the more love one has for him . . .'

Grand Princess Elizaveta Feodorovna and Grand Prince Sergei in Darmstadt in about 1889. This photograph speaks volumes of a couple who stood side by side for over twenty years, no matter what the world said about them. 'People will intrigue and lie as long as the world exists,' Elizaveta told her grandmother in 1896, 'and we are not the first not the last, who have been calumniated.' Their understanding deepened in 1891, when Elizaveta chose to convert to Orthodoxy, having initially opted to keep her Lutheran faith. Like Grand Prince Konstantin, Sergei had found this very difficult but said nothing – 'He was a real angel of kindness . . . never, never did he complain' – and his patience was rewarded. Childlessness was the one enduring sorrow the couple shared and they seem to have known that this would always be the case. Other family members knew it too: 'Poor Sergei and Ella,' Alexander III told his wife in the spring of 1892, '. . . for all their lives they are denied this great blessing.'

From childhood Sergei was close to his younger brother Grand Prince Pavel Alexandrovich – to the extent that Pavel even shared Sergei and Elizaveta's honeymoon. A victim of frequent respiratory disease, Pavel often spent winters in Greece with his cousin Grand Princess Olga Konstantinovna and her family and it was there that he found a bride. Princess Alexandra of Greece (*right*), Olga's daughter, who became Grand Princess Alexandra Georgievna on her marriage in June 1889, was no stranger to Russia or to the imperial family: through visits to her mother's family in Russia and her father's family in Denmark she had known them all her life. She was also Orthodox, so her move north to marry Pavel was not too great an upheaval, though she missed the Greek climate.

Elizaveta Feodorovna and Alexandra Georgievna became like sisters, in a mirror image of the relationship that had always existed between their husbands. Pavel's valet Alexei Volkov described the early days of his master's marriage: 'The newly-weds moved into their palace on the Neva embankment behind the Church of the Annunciation and facing the Corps de la Marine. Their family life flowed by there, peaceful and serene. The first child . . . was born in the palace and the couple's closest and most loved companions at this time were Grand Prince Sergei Alexandrovich and his wife, Grand Princess Elizaveta Feodorovna.'

Grand Princess Alexandra Georgievna with her daughter Maria Pavlovna, who was born on 6/18 April 1890 and christened a month later, with the Tsaritsa Maria Feodorovna and Grand Prince Sergei as her godparents.

Alexandra in 1891 with her mother Grand Princess Olga Konstantinovna, her grandmother Grand Princess Alexandra Iosifovna and her daughter Maria.

The summer of 1889 saw two more family weddings: Grand Prince Peter Nikolaevich married Princess Militsa of Montenegro (*right*) at Peterhof and three weeks later her younger sister Stana (*below*) was pledged to his cousin Georgi, Duke of Leuchtenberg, becoming, in the Russian manner, Anastasia Nikolaevna. The daughters of Prince Nikola of Montenegro, Militsa and Stana and their sisters were taken under imperial patronage for political reasons during the reign of Alexander II and were educated in St Petersburg, at the Smolny Institute. The imperial family welcomed them, on the surface at least, and they were included in family gatherings, but fashionable St Petersburg sneered behind its hands, regarding them as poor relations. To this day the old snobbery colours the way the sisters are presented – unfairly, for they were educated women with minds of their own, perfectly well able to do all that was expected of them.

Anastasia's marriage broke down after some years and in the autumn of 1906 society thrilled to rumours of an affair between her and Grand Prince Nikolai Nikolaevich the younger, Peter's brother. Nikolai was a solitary man who kept his emotions rigidly in check; few members of the family came close to him but he had had a long-standing relationship with the daughter of a city official, Sophie Burenina. In 1892 Alexander III gave him permission to marry her as his legal wife, without official recognition, rights or titles. Then, under pressure from a family deputation led by Grand Prince Vladimir, the Tsar changed his mind; Nikolai bowed to this and went on as before, close only to Peter and Peter's family. Anastasia's marriage ended in divorce in November 1906 and gossip saw her and Nikolai as good as married: in fact, Nicholas II wanted to refuse permission and he agreed to the marriage only on advice from the Holy Synod. The couple married in the Crimea in the spring of 1907, to the outrage of the wider family who felt that the Tsar was showing favouritism to the Nikolaevichi.

Grand Princess Maria Georgievna, who married Grand Prince Georgi Mikhailovich at Corfu on 12 May 1900, was the younger sister of Alexandra Georgievna, Grand Princess Pavel, so her ties with the imperial family were strong from childhood. But she was half-hearted about marrying Georgi Mikhailovich and refused him several times. He pursued her for years. When she finally agreed she made it plain that she was not in love, a situation he was prepared to accept in the hope that she would change; predictably, the marriage was not a success. 'She seemed touched by his devotion', a friend wrote, 'and the fortune he laid at her feet dazzled, but never spoilt her nature.' Then children were born, two daughters, but 'through all this seeming bliss the Grand Duke was not happy. He felt all was not well as he had hoped time would make it. The Grand Duchess for her part seemed to feel more and more that nothing could bring that peace which she had known from the first would never exist in her married life.'

Maria Georgievna with her daughters Nina (*left*) and Ksenia in about 1908. In time it would be the children's health that gave the Grand Princess an excuse to spend extended periods away from Russia – and from her husband.

A generation on from page 44, in 1896 Maria Feodorovna, now Dowager Tsaritsa, holds her granddaughter Grand Princess Olga Nikolaevna, Nicholas II's eldest child. The relationship between Maria Feodorovna and her daughter-in-law Alexandra was never easy, but in the early days they managed a degree of harmony. Maria Feodorovna was staying in the palace when baby Olga was born and she became and remained a loving and indulgent grandmother to the five imperial children.

The rivalry between sisters-in-law Maria Feodorovna (*left*), the Dowager Tsaritsa, and Maria Pavlovna (*below*), Grand Princess Vladimir, lasted into the new reign. Then, what had always been a matter of petty spitefulness between two very confident and well-placed women, neither really intent on hurting the other, became a source of real division. The young Tsaritsa was caught between the two women who might have been most helpful to her in her challenging new role. Unable to feel at ease with her mother-in-law, she also repelled Grand Princess Vladimir's attempts to take her over, creating a lasting resentment. Her isolation within the family increased.

The dress Maria Feodorovna is wearing in this photo survives to this day. Made by the couturier Worth of Paris in maroon velvet with a carnation pattern embroidered in shades of gold, it was included in an exhibition of nineteenth-century costume in the State Hermitage in 1993.

The Vladimirs, on the occasion of their Silver Wedding in 1899; from the left, Grand Prince Andrei, Grand Prince Vladimir, Grand Princess Elena, Grand Prince Kirill, Grand Princess Maria Pavlovna and Grand Prince Boris.

Grand Princess Elizaveta Mavrikievna and Grand Prince Konstantin in a photograph that underlines the long happiness of their married life. Recently, passages extracted from the Grand Prince's diary suggesting homosexual activity have dominated everything written about him. But even if these can be taken at face value they represent only isolated episodes in his life which he himself regretted. The effect of their publication has been to negate the important and consistent part played at his side by one person: Elizaveta, his wife and companion for more than three decades and the mother of their nine children, the births stretching over a twenty-year period. The photograph below was taken on the name day of their youngest son Georgi, 23 April 1909, but it commemorates the Silver Wedding a week earlier. The Grand Prince's diary describes how the family celebration for Georgi at Tsarskoe Selo was followed by a group sitting at Pavlovsk, in the library of the Empress Maria Feodorovna (wife of Tsar Paul), for the photographer Gorodetsky. The photo shows (*from left to right, in uniform*) Prince Igor, Duke Ernst II of Saxe-Altenburg (Elizaveta's brother), Prince Gavril, Grand Prince Konstantin, Prince Ioann, Prince Konstantin, Prince Oleg; (*in front*) Princess Vera, the Grand Princess, Prince Georgi, Princess Tatiana.

Alexandra Iosifovna, Grand Princess Konstantin, the mother of Konstantin Konstantinovich and the last of her generation: after 1909 no one in the family but she could remember the Court of Nicholas I, into which she came as a young bride, and she delighted in telling the younger women how times had changed. 'A famous beauty in her day,' the daughter of one of her ladies remembered, 'she was now a commanding old lady with snow-white hair, beautifully *coiffé*. She had kept a great sense of dress, and her black, tight-fitting *princesse* frocks set off her tall, erect and slim figure. . . . Alexandra Jossiphovna was the old-fashioned type of princess, gracious and smiling, but never forgetting her rank for a moment.'

The last man of the imperial family to contract a legal marriage was Alexandra Iosifovna's grandson Prince Ioann, eldest son of Grand Prince Konstantin. In the summer of 1911 he became engaged to Princess Elena of Serbia, a niece of Grand Princesses Militsa and Anastasia, who had been brought up under their care and educated at the Smolny after losing her mother at an early age. But it was another of the Montenegrin sisters, Elena, Queen of Italy, who oversaw the engagement, taking Elena into her home and inviting Ioann to visit; he surprised everyone by proposing almost immediately. The thought that Ioann might want to marry caused great amusement in the family: he was a tall, rather plain young man, quiet and deeply religious, and had thought of becoming a monk. But his marriage was a love match and he and Elena were happy, his gentleness complementing her fiery nature. While he returned to his duties with the Chevalier Guard, she studied medicine at the University of St Petersburg, only giving up with some reluctance for the birth of their first child.

Born Romanov

A dynasty stands or falls by its children. To have no children – particularly no sons – was one of the worst fates that could strike a royal couple, but the imperial family was blessed, on the whole, with large families and a preponderance of boys. Nicholas I's daughter Olga, Queen of Württemberg, described the moment when her sister-in-law Maria Alexandrovna gave birth to a son, assuring the succession into the next generation: 'On 8 September, the Feast of the Virgin's Birth, Marie brought her first son Nikolai into the world, who would one day inherit the throne. Papa made his three sons kneel by the child's cradle, to swear their loyalty to the future Tsar. . . . We so loved that peaceful time, when the young mother spent six weeks in complete seclusion. How comfortable it was in the room, secluded from the outside world and half-darkened by curtains, where the mother, weak still, but radiant with happiness, lay with her child in her arms.' The challenge for royal parents was to bring a child into a position of such importance and still allow it to be normal. So nursery life tended to be very simple, even in the richest of palaces. Clothes were handed down, the most expensive toys deemed unsuitable for daily use and the youngest Romanovs were rarely addressed by their titles. In an extraordinary setting they shared the experiences common to all children.

When Nicholas II was born in May 1868 (*above, left*), his uncles were not brought in to kneel and pledge their loyalty – in later life he might have wished that they were – but his mother was attended throughout her ordeal by two Tsars, one present and one future, and a Tsaritsa. 'God sent us a son whom we gave the name of Nikolai,' the future Tsar Alexander III wrote in his diary. 'What a joy it was, it is not to be described. I rushed to embrace my darling wife who cheered up at once and was terrifically happy. I was crying like a baby.'

(*Above, right*) Nicholas II's cousin Maria Pavlovna the younger, daughter of his uncle Pavel, born in 1890.

(*Left*) His third daughter Maria Nikolaevna, who was born in the Alexandria Dacha at Peterhof in 1899. Three pairs of white horses took her to her christening in a gilt and glass carriage, attended by grooms in white and scarlet livery and a Cossack escort. The Grand Mistress of the Court, Princess Golitsina, carried her into the chapel on a pillow of cloth-of-gold – but under her robes the baby wore the simple infant shirt that her father had worn on the day he was christened.

No birth was awaited or despaired of quite like that of the Tsesarevich Alexei (*right*), and the ceremony at his christening outshone even that arranged for his sisters. Four pairs of horses drew his carriage and almost the whole imperial family, including the children dressed in full Court dress and uniform, all in miniature, turned out to watch. His godfathers included the Kings of England and Denmark, Kaiser Wilhelm II and Grand Prince Alexei Alexandrovich, his great-uncle. Princess Golitsina was still responsible for the baby's entry into the chapel. Five years older now, she was desperately afraid of dropping her precious load, so, to reassure her, broad ribbons were sewn to the cushion and secured around her neck. This cushion, still with its supporting ribbons, and Alexei's long christening gown are displayed today in the Alexander Palace at Tsarskoe Selo. The imperial nursery used also to boast a silver bath, bought in 1796 for the infant Nicholas I and engraved with the name of every child in the main line of the family since that time.

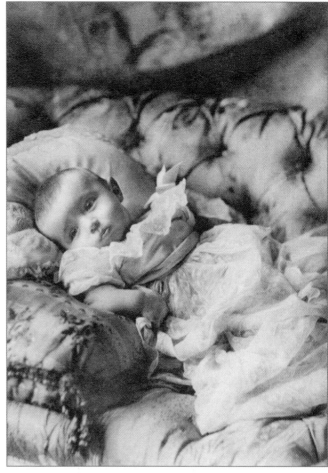

One of the last Romanov babies to be born before the Revolution was Vsevelod Ioannovich (*left*), the first child of Ioann Konstantinovich and Elena of Serbia, who was born at Pavlovsk in January 1914. Vsevelod was only of minor importance in the family, being the great-great-grandson of a Tsar, but his grandfather was the King of Serbia and, as 1914 progressed, the relationship with that country began to loom large in the Russian mind. So he was given a christening appropriate to the moment, with the Tsar as his godfather, both Tsaritsas and the whole imperial family in attendance. He was an attractive child, and much loved. The writer E.M. Almedingen remembered an incident that happened during Prince Ioann's last visit to her school. It was in the spring of 1916 and some of the girls stopped the Prince to ask about the progress of the war. 'Then he moved away, turned at the door, smiled, and looked very much like a boy on his birthday. "Oh I would like to tell you that my son cut his first tooth a few days ago."'

Princess Irina Alexandrovna, daughter of Grand Prince Alexander Mikhailovich and Grand Princess Ksenia, in 1896: 'Baby is growing up wonderfully,' her mother commented in the September of that year. 'Now if you stand her on her feet, she can remain there a few seconds without any help; she is already trying to take a few steps, which amuses her greatly, and is constantly asking to be put on the floor!'

Princess Vera Konstantinovna, youngest child of Grand Prince Konstantin Konstantinovich, in about 1908/9. It is always said that the last Tsar's children led a very isolated life, shut away from the rest of the family. In fact, they did have contact with their cousins: this extract from Grand Prince Konstantin's diary describes a typical tea-party in November 1908 and, young as she was, Princess Vera was included: 'Our little ones were invited to tea with the Emperor's children. Igor went too. Little Anastasia was thrilled with him, kept calling him a nice little boy and gave him flowers when they said goodbye. The Heir, who is a year younger that Georgy, hugged him and played happily with him on the slide, and on learning that Georgy wants to be a chauffeur when he grows up, offered his services as his assistant. The girls made a fuss of our Vera and carried her in their arms.'

Princess Irina in 1898 with her brother Prince Andrei; not long before this photo was taken, the children's uncle Nicholas II had described them in a letter to his brother Georgi, anticipating what would happen when Irina and Andrei came together with his own little girls: 'The one amusing event will be the meeting of our two daughters – Olga and Irina. I can just see them pulling each other's hair and quarrelling over the toys. I still can't believe that Xenia is the mother of two children! Her Andrusha is a big, healthy boy, but still very ugly; please don't you tell her that.'

Maria Pavlovna the younger (*right*) described the delights of a palace Christmas: 'Days before, the trees would be brought out and set up. Then the doors of the great reception hall would be closed; then mysterious preparations, half sensed, would go forward all around us. . . . Finally the great moment came. When we were dressed father came for us. He led us to the doors of the closed reception hall and made a sign. The electric lights within the large room were snapped off, the doors thrown open. Before our enchanted eyes appeared, in that immense dark room, the magic trees, ablaze with candles. Our hearts stopped beating, and tremblingly we entered after our father. He made another sign; darkness vanished; along the walls appeared tables covered with white cloths and on these tables were the gifts.'

Prince Ioann as a child (*centre*) with his father Grand Prince Konstantin and brother Gavril in about 1890. Ioann Konstantinovich was the first member of the imperial family to be three generations removed from a reigning Tsar. His parents' marriage and the prospect of children prompted Alexander III to make a decision which, however necessary, was not popular. For generations, every legitimate child in the family had borne the title '*Velikii Kniaz*' [Grand Prince] or '*Velikii Kniazhna*' [Grand Princess], with a guaranteed income on attaining their majority. It confirmed their status and acknowledged how much would be expected of them. But the family was growing. In January 1885 Alexander III announced a limitation of the existing titles to the Tsar's children and grandchildren. The next generation would be '*Kniaz*' or '*Kniazhna*' [Prince or Princess], 'Highness' instead of 'Imperial Highness', with a reduced income. Elizaveta Mavrikievna told her father, 'At first I was very angry, but now I say, far better a good <u>Kniaz</u> than a good-for-nothing <u>Velikii Kniaz</u>.' She blamed the change on the Mikhails for having so many sons. The decision became law within days of Ioann's birth.

Despite wealth and titles, the children were children still and enjoyed very simple things – like the rough wooden cart in the photo above and the cloth elephant, obviously home-made and well loved. Grand Princes Boris and Andrei Vladimirovich (*right*), taken here by Levitsky in about 1881/2, have an equally simple sleigh-on-wheels which probably had a cord or handle so that it could be pulled along. This photograph captures some of the rites-of-passage of boyhood: Boris (*standing*), at three or four years old, has been promoted to trousers though he still has very long hair. Andrei's hair appears to have been cut, but he wears the skirt common to toddlers of both sexes.

At five or six years old when this photo was taken, Grand Prince Mikhail Alexandrovich, Alexander III's youngest son (*right*), was rather grown-up for a skirt, but his mother Maria Feodorovna liked to keep her children young and Mikhail was a family pet: 'Little Micha is so sweet and affectionate and could <u>almost</u> be my favourite if I were not against making any difference,' she told her father, about a year before this was taken. 'I love all of them alike, but each in his own way.' The pose, however, is entirely adult and the magnificent horse and miniature breastplate and helmet anticipate Mikhail's future as a cavalry officer.

Grand Princess Olga Nikolaevna, Nicholas II's eldest child, with a clown doll in 1898. In November 1896 her aunt Ksenia described a visit to the palace: 'Before tea we went into the nursery. Nicky and Alix sat in the play pen and played with their daughter! She is a splendid, huge little girl, and seems to have got prettier, taller and even fatter! She was too sweet with us!' Many of the toys of the last Tsar's children are now displayed in the toy museum at Zagorsk, where the guides explain that they had some toys to play with and others that were far too valuable for everyday use.

A photograph which encapsulates everything that might set a royal child apart. For tea outdoors, little Maria Pavlovna and her brother Dmitri sit in their high chairs on a carpet, with their uniformed English nurses, Mrs Fry (*in front of the table*) and Lizzie Grove, to keep order. The samovar stands on a starched white table cloth and two liveried servants complete the picture. Fortunately, most family picnics were much more relaxed than this and sitting on the grass was a delight the children were not always forbidden.

Grand Prince Dmitri (*right, in the tartan sash, with his sister*) was a seven-month baby, born as his mother lapsed into a fatal coma. They thought him dead, and he owed his life to Mrs Fry who noticed movement within the discarded bundle of blankets. But long before the days of incubators and specialist baby care units it was hard to sustain life in a premature baby. Dmitri had to be wrapped in cotton wool – literally – and kept warm with hot water bottles. The doctors also prescribed special warm baths. It was the baby's uncle, Grand Prince Sergei Alexandrovich, who took on the delicate task of caring for Dmitri personally until the first weeks were safely over.

English nurses like Mrs Fry had managed the imperial nurseries ever since Nicholas I was a baby – perhaps earlier. When Alexander III and Maria Feodorovna's youngest child Olga (*right, with her elder sister Ksenia*) proved to be delicate enquiries were made through her aunt Alexandra, Princess of Wales, and an experienced English nurse was approached. Mrs Elizabeth Franklin was respected in London society. It was her particular skill to take on a sickly baby and stay in the home only for the time it took to bring the infant to full health. Her invitation from the Tsaritsa was an honour she was pleased to accept. She left for Russia in the spring of 1883 expecting to stay only a limited time; in fact, she stayed for life, becoming indispensable to Olga and far closer to the child than her own mother. Even as a married woman, Olga still took notice of 'Nana'. Mrs Franklin died in Olga's marital home on Sergeevskaya Street, St Petersburg, in April 1913 and was given an appreciative obituary in the Russian press.

Andrei, Kirill and Boris Vladimirovich and their sister Elena, the children of Grand Prince Vladimir, in the late 1880s. Despite the German sympathies of their parents, these children too had an English nurse, Millicent Crofts, whose aunt had nursed their father and his siblings. 'Milly was with us from our earliest days,' Kirill remembered, 'and it was through her that the first language we talked was English. I can remember her singing nursery rhymes to us; later she introduced us to the works of English literature, the first of which were *Barnaby Rudge* and *Oliver Twist*.'

(*Above*) Princess Marina and Prince Roman, elder children of Grand Prince Peter Nikolaevich, in about 1899. Marina and Roman had an English governess, Mrs Taylor, and a rather unusual nurse. They called her 'Mascha' and she was born and raised, like her father before her, on their family's estates. 'With us children she shared joy and sorrow,' Roman remembered. 'She was always our trusted friend, in Russia and the same later in exile.' He recalled her characteristic greeting to his father – a kiss on the left shoulder. His uncle Nikolai was so tall that she had to kiss his arm. She had known them all her life.

(*Left*) Grand Prince Konstantin Konstantinovich's children, Tatiana, Oleg, baby Igor and Konstantin with their German nurse, Angelika Klein – the children called her 'Ika' – in 1895. Prince Igor was blue at birth from lack of oxygen and had to be swung vigorously to force air into his lungs. Prince Roman – who was close to him when both were in their teens – remembered him as a lively, argumentative boy, often told off for speaking too loudly. Prince Oleg (*in front*) was gifted with an interest in everything around him and with boundless imagination. He led the other children, older and younger, in complex fantasy games of his own devising.

Nurses apart, the imperial children also had frequent contact with the Cossacks and soldiers of the Guards regiments and sailors of the imperial yacht who were detailed to watch over them. In 1897 Nicholas II told his mother, 'The cossacks, soldiers and negroes are Olga's greatest friends, and she greets them as she goes down the corridor.' This photograph, taken on the lawns at Alexandria Peterhof in 1900, shows Olga and her sisters Tatiana and Maria with one of the soldiers of the escort. The soldiers regarded the children with awed respect. Margaretta Eagar, who was nursery governess to Nicholas II's four daughters, recalled how one officer had some shiny pebbles the children gave him mounted on to his watch chain, another begged a doll from them and a third told her 'he was in some trouble, and seeing the children coming out, thought that if he could reach the carriage in time to bow to the children he would find a way out of his troubles'.

Olga (*left*) and Tatiana together at about the same time, taken by Hahn.

Alexander II's children Maria and Sergei in 1861. They too had an English nurse, Kitty Strutton, who was employed when the future Alexander III was born and looked after each of the younger children in turn. But overall charge of the nurseries, and of Maria Alexandrovna until her marriage, was given to a noblewoman, Countess Alexandra Tolstoy. She was a remarkable character: tough, uncompromising and loving. In later years one of Maria's daughters recalled her in old age: 'Her appearance in our midst, in Russia or elsewhere, was as a trumpet call to order. During her "occupation" of the house (for no other word rightly expresses her attitude), everybody would be on their mettle, no lukewarmness was tolerated or even possible. . . . But I believe that although in awe of her, Mamma loved her old governess very dearly; she was a strong link with the past, with the beloved home. . . . I think she had a heart of gold; she loved us dearly and I can still well recall the sensation of being buried, so to say, in her ample chins, whilst she clasped us in a grandmotherly embrace.'

A strikingly adult portrait of little Anastasia Mikhailovna, Maria Alexandrovna's cousin, in about 1864. Anastasia spent most of her formative years in the Viceregal palaces in the Caucasus, as the only sister of six lively brothers. Her mother, Grand Princess Olga Feodorovna, was renowned for her strictness to her children – at least in their own accounts and in the memories of those who knew them well. 'It was characteristic of the small amount of self-determination which my mother had as a girl', Anastasia's daughter remembered, 'that although she owned an apricot tree in the garden at Borjom, my grandfather's country seat, she was not allowed to enjoy the juicy, sun-drenched fruit without explicit permission.' The words of Anastasia's mother and her governess were law, admitting no argument.

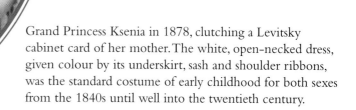

Grand Princess Ksenia in 1878, clutching a Levitsky cabinet card of her mother. The white, open-necked dress, given colour by its underskirt, sash and shoulder ribbons, was the standard costume of early childhood for both sexes from the 1840s until well into the twentieth century.

Three Grand Princes, Sergei Alexandrovich (*above left, in 1861*), Mikhail Mikhailovich (*above right, in about 1866*) and his brother Sergei Mikhailovich (*right, in about 1875*), wearing the loose Russian shirt with a side fastening that was almost a uniform for the younger boys of the family from the 1820s to the 1870s, and was still worn occasionally into the next century. Around the 1840s and 1850s this set the fashion for little boys across Europe but it was native to Russia; after his accession, Alexander III had the everyday uniforms of the Russian army redesigned on this pattern, so that the Russian shirt also came to be worn by the men of the family. Alexander was fond of it himself and so, in later years, was Nicholas II.

Two photographs that span a generation: (*right*) Grand Prince Peter Nikolaevich in 1868 and (*below*) his son Prince Roman in 1899, both wearing variations of Russian costume. Grand Prince Peter had a lonely childhood. With only one brother, who was eight years older than himself, and parents who did not get on, Peter spent long periods with only nurses, tutors and servants. In the late 1870s, with his father and brother away at the Turkish War and his mother setting up home in Kiev, Peter was taken into the Winter Palace by Alexander II; there he made friends with the other boys of the family too young to fight, Dmitri Konstantinovich and Pavel Alexandrovich, who were both five years older than himself, and Georgi and Alexander Mikhailovich. They rode penny-farthing bicycles through the vast state rooms and, when the Tsar was not at the front, took morning tea with him in his study. Peter became especially close to Georgi Mikhailovich, a friendship which lasted the rest of their lives.

With two sisters, one older and one younger, and loving parents, Prince Roman's childhood was less solitary. A regular playmate of Nicholas II's daughters, he recalled an early meeting with their great-grandmother, Queen Victoria, on the Riviera. She called on his parents but they were not at home, 'and the Queen went into the garden to greet Marina and myself. My sister kissed the Queen's hand, as any well-brought-up five-year-old would. I, on the other hand, in my pram, met her with complete indifference and, as the Queen bent over the pram, stuck out my foot without respect, for her to kiss!'

Despite the extraordinary frock and lace knickers, the smaller child here is a boy, Grand Prince Georgi Alexandrovich, pictured in around 1873. The elaborate outfit worn by the future Tsar Nicholas II here is also unusual: these must surely have been party clothes for two boys whose normal wear was the plain sailor suit, in white drill for the summer, navy serge for winter. The Russian shirt still worn by their cousins – Nicholas and Sergei Mikhailovich were very much of an age – seems to have passed by the sons of Maria Feodorovna and Alexander III, whose clothes, in photographs at least, were always much more western.

The English-style sailor suit arrived at the
Russian Court with the children of the Tsarevna
Maria Feodorovna and of Maria Pavlovna,
Grand Princess Vladimir, and by the end of the
nineteenth century it was universal. These
children are (*above*), Princes Nikita, Andrei,
Feodor (*in front*), Rostislav, Dmitri (*in front*) and
Princess Irina, the family of Grand Princess
Ksenia. (*Right*) Prince Georgi Konstantinovich –
whose plan to become a chauffeur won such
enthusiastic support from the Tsesarevich Alexei.

Another pair of photographs that spans the generations: (*above left*) Grand Princes Dmitri, Konstantin and Viacheslav Konstantinovich, dressed for the Russian winter in about 1866 – at about eight or nine years old Konstantin, the eldest, has already gone into uniform; (*above right*) three of Konstantin's children, Tatiana, Konstantin and Oleg, in winter coats about thirty years later: the dark coat and hat young Konstantin is wearing are very similar in style to those of his younger uncles.

Grand Princesses Olga and Tatiana Nikolaevna in 1900, wearing summer coats and hats.

5

The Training of Princes

Every Romanov prince was attached to a regiment at birth. As a man, he would be expected to see himself as an officer constantly on active service and to wear uniform at all times. But in reality, the miniature uniforms and weapons given to the princes in childhood were only a reminder of the future and a mark of rank. First came the long years of education, following a pattern that hardly varied for generations. All imperial children received their first lessons from women. At about seven years old the boys moved on to an all-male environment, with civilian tutors under the supervision of a military governor and lessons which included elements of military training. Most studied at home, with only brothers, cousins or hand-picked classmates, but a few experienced school life, in St Petersburg's Corps des Pages or the regimental cadet schools. In their mid-teens the serious military training began. Officially a prince had to enter the armed forces, but a few were lucky enough to bend the mould to fit their individual talents. Their sisters remained under the supervision of women, but female education was prized in Russia and the girls were often taught by the same tutors as their brothers. They were groomed to appear in public and to perform ceremonial duties appropriate to their sex and age.

The Tsesarevich Nikolai in about 1856. At thirteen years old Nikolai performed one of his first official duties before the Court: 'The Heir was godfather at the christening of his little brother Sergei,' Anna Tiutcheva wrote, 'and he played his part with great dignity and skill.' A heavy weight of expectation rested on Nikolai and his education was intense. Lessons kept him at home while his mother and the younger children travelled – babies excepted. A few months after the christening, the family went to Germany without Nikolai. 'Dearest Mama,' he wrote from Peterhof, 'I thank you very much for the wonderful book you sent me; I have already looked through the book with my tutor too. . . . I have seen a letter from Alexei to Papa, where he says that he has seen a snake but does not say where. The State Courier who arrived yesterday brought us regards and complaints from Alexei, that we don't write to him enough. We found it very funny. Seriozha, I think, has grown up and is becoming very nice. We saw him yesterday in the bath. I am beginning to paint in oils and I'm working now on a drawing for Papa. I hope you're well, dear Mama, I kiss you, Seichik, Mary, Uncle Alexander and all of you. . .'

Nikolai's brothers, Grand Princes Alexander (*left*) and Vladimir. Alexander III was, and still is, often dismissed as a man of limited intelligence educated only for the army. It is certainly true that his parents concentrated most of their efforts on Nikolai, but Alexander was also taught by academics of very high calibre – men like Prince Bestuzhev-Ryumin, founder of Russia's first higher educational institution for women and Professor Chivelev, an economist from the University of Moscow. Alexander developed a passion for archaeology, history and Russian art; while he was still in his teens his enthusiasm became the driving force behind the creation of the Russian Historical Society. He also helped in the compilation of the *Russian Biographical Encyclopaedia*.

Sometimes education was tailored to individual needs. Grand Prince Sergei (*right*) was not quite eight years old when Nikolai died and the tragedy affected him badly. His mother was so anxious that she called on a trusted clergyman, Abbot Leonid of the Savvino-Storozhevsk Monastery, to help him. Abbot Leonid became a mentor to Sergei and had a profound influence on him. Many of Sergei's lessons were shared with his cousin, Grand Prince Konstantin Konstantinovich (*below left*), and the two grew up as deeply religious, highly cultured men and friends for life. Konstantin wrote poetry from childhood and would become a published poet under the initials 'KR'. Sergei taught himself Italian in order to read Dante in the original. The writer Dostoevsky knew them both and was drawn into the later stages of their education.

A less creditable story is told of the tutor of Grand Prince Viacheslav (*below right*), Konstantin's youngest brother. Their mother travelled a lot and liked to take Viacheslav with her. His tutor, a Cossack NCO, accompanied him until an unfortunate incident in Leipzig in 1868/9. The tutor drank too much in a tavern and some students, finding him insensible, carried him off to a fairground and put him on show for money, in full Cossack uniform, with a placard tied round his neck.

Grand Princes Nicholas and Georgi, the elder sons of Alexander III, in about 1886. As part of their education the brothers learned English from Charles Heath, who had also taught their uncles Sergei and Pavel. The writer W. T. Stead remembered Heath as 'an English gentleman in the best sense of the word, simple, unaffected, frank, straightforward, and manly', who came to the imperial family from a teaching post in the Alexander Lyceum at Tsarskoe Selo, which boasted the poet Alexander Pushkin as a former pupil. Nicholas liked Heath and was strongly influenced by him. Georgi, who was an incorrigible practical joker, tormented the tutor with his pet parrot 'Popka', which had been trained to speak with an exaggerated British accent.

Grand Prince Mikhail Alexandrovich, their younger brother, became particularly close to their Swiss tutor Ferdinand Thormeyer. 'If you do not come to me I will not sleep,' the little boy wrote from Peterhof in one of his childhood notes, 'Come quickly.' Thormeyer joined the household of Alexander III in the mid-1880s and taught all the Tsar's children. His subject was French, but his diaries show that he played a much wider role in the children's lives. When Mikhail became his pupil at seven years old, Thormeyer took him for walks, assisted in his dancing and music lessons and joined in his games, while still teaching the older children. They called him 'Siocha'. Long after his appointment ended he kept in touch with his former pupils, exchanging letters and gifts, and the affection between them remained.

In terms of education, the most remarkable household within the imperial family was that of Grand Prince Konstantin Konstantinovich. He was a remarkable man; poet, dramatist, musician, scientist and soldier, and he ensured that his children were exposed to the very best in all disciplines. 'Famous archaeologists told us about the newest excavations . . . . an Eastern traveller would tell us about the magic of Samarkand, and exhibit tiles in glowing blues and yellows . . . we listened to long-bearded

choirs of Old Believers singing sixteenth century Church music. Peasants from different provinces came to sing the old popular songs. Famous architects showed us slides and explained . . . buildings from all parts of the empire.' The photo above shows the family on 17 August 1900: (*from the right*) the Grand Prince, Grand Princess Elizaveta Mavrikievna, Princes Ioann and Gavril, Princess Tatiana, Princes Konstantin, Oleg and Igor. None of the children embodied their father's hopes or reflected his talents so closely as Prince Oleg (*left*), who was quick, intuitive and clever. Like his father, he wrote poetry from childhood and the Grand Prince decided that for him a conventional military education would not be appropriate. He sent Oleg to the Alexander Lyceum – arousing the disapproval of the other men in the imperial family.

For the first twelve years of his life Nicholas II was two generations removed from the throne, which enabled him to grow up in comparative peace. His own son Alexei (*left*), being born 'in the purple', could never be so sheltered from public and Court attention, and the Tsar tried to give him the best preparation possible for his future role. Before he could walk, Alexei was carried in his father's arms at troop reviews. As a toddler he sampled the food served to sailors on the imperial yacht and shook hands with lines of dignitaries. A child-sized table in the Tsar's study at the Alexander Palace enabled him to sit in on the meetings and audiences which were a regular part of his father's day.

Alexei with his tutor, Piotr Vasilievich Petrov, an official of the Military Training Institutions who taught Russian literature and language to all of the last Tsar's children and was a great favourite with them. Petrov was separated from the family early in 1917, but he kept in touch with the children and with their other tutors by letter. Though he remained in Russia after the Revolution he treasured these letters, with photographs, drawings by the children and other souvenirs, carefully annotated in his own archive. This is now preserved in the collections of the State Archive of the Russian Federation.

The military element in the lives of the Grand Princes began even before their first lessons. Grand Prince Nikolai Nikolaevich the younger (*right, in about 1867*) was born on 6/18 November, the feast day of the Guard Hussars. His uncle, Alexander II, visited him as soon as the regimental celebration was over and hung the regiment's insignia on the cradle. A lonely boy, who remained something of an outsider in the family, Nikolai Nikolaevich learned from an unhappy home life to hide his feelings. Emotion embarrassed him. He was taught by military tutors and immersed himself in military studies, preparing for entry to the Nikolaevsky Engineering Academy when he was sixteen. The army was his first real home and he relished both the life and the studies at the Academy, becoming an outstanding student. His training was completed at the General Staff Academy.

His cousin, Grand Prince Nikolai Mikhailovich, had a very Spartan upbringing. As the eldest of the six sons of the Viceroy of the Caucasus, Nikolai was the first to experience its full rigours; his younger brother Alexander would later remember how the presentation of a full officer's uniform, with sword, on his seventh birthday was followed by removal to the barrack-like quarters where Nikolai, Mikhail and Georgi already lived. No luxury was allowed them and the discipline that governed their days was harsh – yet, unlike Nikolai Nikolaevich, they were not lonely. The Mikhailovich Princes were an intelligent, articulate and very self-sufficient group and, as the eldest, Nikolai led the pack. When he went on to the General Staff Academy he found himself a few years behind Nikolai Nikolaevich – he found, too, that his cousin was successful and he suffered by comparison – and this fired a jealousy of Nikolai Nikolaevich and an animosity towards him that grew with the years.

Grand Prince Pavel Alexandrovich in Hussar uniform in about 1868. Pavel served with the Grodno Hussars. He was entered on the lists of the 79th Kurinsky Regiment of Infantry while still in his cradle, and as an adult would also command the Cavalry Guard.

(*Right*) Pavel's son, Grand Prince Dmitri, in April 1905, when he was named Commander of the 2nd Battalion of the Tsarskoeselsky Sharpshooters – at the age of thirteen.
(*Below left*) Tsesarevich Alexei in 1911, in the uniform of the Life Guard Strelskovo Regiment of the Imperial Family.
(*Below right*) Alexei in the Alexander Park at Tsarskoe Selo in 1910, wearing the new uniform and equipment of a private soldier in the Russian army.

All Grand Princes held military rank but not all were destined to serve in the army. Nicholas I had his second son Konstantin groomed from childhood for the role of Admiral General of the Russian Navy, and Alexander II followed suit, selecting his fourth son Alexei Alexandrovich for naval training. In this photograph Alexei wears the uniform of a Russian naval rating. (The striped shirt worn by later Russian sailors and in use to this day was introduced by his uncle Konstantin, the Admiral General.) The photo was taken in 1860 – the year in which Alexei and his cousin Nikolai Konstantinovich (*below*) took part in their first naval manoeuvres in the Baltic, at the age of ten. They were at sea for a little over two weeks.

Grand Prince Nikolai Konstantinovich was the eldest son of the Admiral General. He and Alexei were born only four weeks apart, and when Alexei received his first naval dress uniform in January 1857 the Admiral General told the Tsar, 'The officer's dress uniform given to Alexei on his seventh birthday excited not a little envy, but he [Nikolai] comforts himself with the thought that soon he too will be favoured. It will be nice to see both our little sailors in identical dress uniforms.' The two boys made their first communion together, and shared their education and their training. In 1861 they had their second experience of life at sea in the yacht *Zabavu*, cruising the Finnish skerries.

Grand Prince Alexei and his suite, in a group taken around the time of his coming-of-age in 1866. By the end of the 1860s Alexei was a naval lieutenant serving on the frigate *Svetlana*. In 1871 his father sent him on a state visit to America in response to an invitation from President Grant. While there he made an extensive tour, hunted buffalo with General Custer and 'Buffalo' Bill Cody and sailed down the Mississippi on a river boat. It was said that he broke scores of hearts on the way, but he told his parents, 'I can honestly say that this is complete nonsense. They look at me as people look at a caged crocodile . . . but then, having looked me over, become completely indifferent.'

Grand Prince Konstantin Nikolaevich was not content to have one son in the navy but entered each of his sons for training in turn. Konstantin Konstantinovich began his naval service in the 1870s, when his cousin Alexei had risen to command of the *Svetlana*. (Nikolai Konstantinovich by this time had persuaded his father to let him leave the sea and serve in the army.) Lady Augusta Stanley, visiting the Russian Court with her husband on behalf of Queen Victoria in 1874, sat next to Konstantin Konstantinovich at a banquet and found him 'an enchanting companion . . . a very young sailor very clever and quite "un homme du monde". I suppose about fifteen or less and very good looking and most conversible.' Konstantin travelled widely on *Svetlana* before persuading his father that he too was more suited to life on land.

Grand Prince Alexander Mikhailovich claimed to have chosen a naval career for himself, his imagination fired by stories of travel and the promise of escape. His parents were not happy with the idea but Alexander III gave it his blessing. 'How clearly I can see the day when I left our summer palace of Michailovsky to start the career of a sailor. Our small chapel was packed with relatives, aides-de-camp, and servants, and when the deep-voiced priest presented me with an ikon at the conclusion of the Te Deum, my mother began to cry. . . . Feeling the ribbons of my sailor's cap flutter gently about my face and casting an admiring glance at my wide black trousers, I went perfunctorily through the ritual of kissing. My heart was already far away. . . . I was as gay as a prisoner at the dawn of his last day in jail.' The photograph was taken in Sweden on one of Alexander's first Baltic cruises: he would have been about sixteen years old.

Grand Prince Kirill Vladimirovich was destined for the Navy from childhood. This photograph dates from the mid-1880s and shows him in army uniform; his serious naval training did not begin until he was fifteen, when he started to follow the syllabus of the Naval College in his palace classroom. His memories of his first training ship were a world away from those of Alexander Mikhailovich: 'before anything could be done on that hulk of a frigate . . . there had to precede a storm of vehement abuse, without which no yard could be squared and no sail trimmed. This flow of dirt, for it was nothing but the uttermost filth, resounded from morning till night, accompanied by the savage outbursts of violence on the part of our commander. . . . This is what came to my ears, and it was fortunate, indeed, that much of it was lost to me, I who had scarcely ever heard an angry word spoken.'

The future Tsar Nicholas II in about 1889 in the uniform of His Imperial Majesty's Own Convoy, a regiment formed in 1811 from regional Cossack battalions. From 1894 Nicholas commanded the Convoy. His regimental training, which began in the summer of 1884 with the Combined Regiment of the Guard and continued in the Preobrajensky Regiment and the Guard Hussars, was the happiest and least pressured time of his life. 'I am now happier than I can say to have joined the army,' he told his mother from camp at Krasnoe Selo in the summer of 1887, 'and every day I become more and more used to camp life.' After his accession he missed the life desperately, telling his brother, 'before all my thoughts were focused on military service . . . it was the one thing I adored and to it alone I was totally dedicated! Apart from anything else, the knowledge that I am forever cut off from a life close to the armed forces – adds no little sorrow to my burden.'

Prince Ioann Konstantinovich in the uniform of the Cavalry Guard. On 14 June 1907 Ioann and his brother Gavril (*below*) graduated with other cadets of the military training schools and received officer's rank in a passing-out parade presided over by Nicholas II and attended by their parents and their aunt, Grand Princess Olga Konstantinovna, Queen of the Hellenes. 'Believe in God and never lose courage,' the Tsar told them. 'Devote yourselves to the throne and to your duty . . . In your relationships with those you command be strict but fair. Take care of their interests and their needs and they will repay you a hundred-fold . . . The strength of any military organisation rests in the solidity of the bond between officers and men . . .' Ioann was gazetted to the Cavalry Guard and Gavril to the Guard Hussars and, once the announcement was made, the brothers made their way to their uncle Dmitri's room in the barracks to put on their new uniforms and the insignia of the various orders granted to all princes of the family on their coming-of-age.

It was a proud moment. Gavril in particular had lived for the army since he was a small boy. From 1900 to 1902 he was a cadet in the First Moscow Corps. In 1903, at the age of sixteen, he entered cavalry school and would later remember the moment with artless enthusiasm: 'From the age of seven I had dreamed of entering the Nikolaevsky Cavalry School and at last my dream came true! After wearing a cadet uniform for five years I became a real military man at last . . . What happiness it was to put on a cavalry sword!'

For girls things were altogether different. Grand Princess Maria Alexandrovna (*right, with her mother the Tsaritsa in 1867*) was educated at home under the supervision of her formidable governess Countess Tolstoy and was groomed for marriage, like every other princess of her day, though her parents were reluctant to let her go; Lady Augusta Stanley was told that she had been 'a *friend* as well as a daughter – and that her Mother quite leant on her for all sorts of decisions'. Maria was very musical and a piano her father gave her when she was still very small occupied pride of place in her rooms. On long journeys she gave music lessons to her younger brothers, Sergei and Pavel – a task she took very seriously. She mothered them in many ways, and took their interests to heart.

Maria's cousin, Grand Princess Vera Konstantinovna, with her aunt Olga, Queen of Württemberg. The younger daughter of the Admiral-General, Vera spent a large part of her childhood with her aunt in Stuttgart. She is said to have suffered from a nervous condition, possibly something akin to St Vitus' Dance, possibly epilepsy, which was not well understood in the family. 'As a child,' her niece, Princess Marie of Greece, recalled, she 'had been extremely nervous and difficult to manage; her mother . . . sent her to her sister-in-law, Queen Olga of Württemberg, who kept her and educated her and loved her as her own daughter, having no children of her own.'

Grand Princess Elena Vladimirovna, Grand Prince Kirill's sister (*left*), was apparently rather wild. The painter Henry Jones Thaddeus recalled an incident in the spring of 1886 when Elena, as a four-year-old, was brought to him for a sitting. He noticed that she was in a temper with her nurse: 'suddenly she seized a large paper-knife from a table near and made a lunge at the nurse, who, retreating before the onslaught, took refuge behind me. The little lady then transferred her attention to me, her black eyes ablaze with fury . . .' She was a pretty girl, raised by an ambitious mother to be aware at all times of who and what she was. 'Poor little thing, I feel sorry for her,' wrote the Dowager Tsaritsa Maria Feodorovna, her mother's old rival, 'for she is really quite sweet, but vain and pretty grandiose.'

(*Below*) Maria Feodorovna's own younger daughter, Grand Princess Olga Alexandrovna, at Gatchina with her dolls. Olga could not have been more different from her cousin Elena. Simple things appealed to her as they did to her father. She adored him, her brothers – particularly Mikhail, her constant companion – her pets and her nurse. She had no governess and classroom work left her cold – except drawing, for which she had a real talent.

Appearances at Court were part of the training of a princess. Maria Pavlovna the younger (*right*) wears a child's version of the formal dress worn by the ladies of the Court. The photograph was taken around 1901 – possibly for the christening of Anastasia Nikolaevna. Tatiana and Olga Nikolaevna (*above right*) and Tatiana Konstantinovna (*above left*) are pictured in the costumes they wore for the christening of the Tsesarevich Alexei in the summer of 1904. For the elder daughters of Nicholas II it was a new experience: 'Delightful fair-haired little girls of nine and seven, they . . . had tiny *kakochniks* on their heads, the red ribbon of St Catherine was worn across their shoulders, and each had a miniature diamond star of the order. They had evidently been told to be good on their first appearance in full gala. They were as solemn as judges, and allowed themselves to relax into a smile only when they passed a group of still smaller children, their two tiny sisters and several little cousins, standing near a doorway and gazing open-mouthed as the procession passed.'

Princesses had regimental duties too, which took them far from the routine of their daily lives. Attachment to a particular regiment as patron enabled them to receive deputations of men from their regiments and to ride in review. Maria Alexandrovna, taken in the early 1870s, wears the uniform of the Yamburgsk Uhlans.

Olga (*left*) and Tatiana Nikolaevna in 1911 in the full dress uniforms of the 3rd Elizavetgradsky Hussars (Olga) and the 8th Voznesensky Uhlans (Tatiana). Olga became commander-in-chief of her battalion on 11 July 1909. One of the joys of the position, for a girl, was the right to embellish the uniform, and in 1911 Olga added short white cloaks, lined with fur, to the bright blue tunic and red trousers of the Elizavetgradsky Hussars. Both uniforms survive, though it is curious to note that the uniform often exhibited and illustrated as belonging to Tatiana is dark blue, with cuffs, piping and front panel in a contrasting bright yellow. In the photograph, however, the distinguishing facings are noticeably darker than the main body of the uniform.

6

A Suitable Marriage

After education came marriage. The statutes imposed by Tsar Paul committed his descendants to marry partners of equal birth – limiting their choice to the reigning and former reigning families of Europe. There were also religious considerations: the Orthodox Church forbade marriage between first cousins – normal practice in other dynasties – and, until 1874, foreign princesses who married Romanov men had to convert to Orthodoxy. This continued to apply to the wife of the Heir. The Grand Princesses, on the other hand, would never convert; they remained Orthodox no matter whom they married and, to this day, small Russian churches dotted across Europe recall the daughters and granddaughters of Tsars, given in marriage to foreign princes. These young women rarely transplanted well. With so strong a cultural presence surrounding them in their new countries, almost all remained emphatically Russian and longed for home.

For their brothers, things were even harder. Young men were not sheltered from society. Inevitably their feelings would be stirred first by some pretty maid-of-honour or dancer – making it harder for them to settle to a 'suitable' arrangement; and as the family tree spread and grew the chances of finding suitable partners for them all shrank to infinity. No single issue caused more heartache to the imperial family than this one, and the casualties of the Family Statutes multiplied down the years.

Grand Princess Maria Alexandrovna was especially close to her father Alexander II: 'We lost our eldest girl and we had so ardently wished for another – her birth was a joy and a delight . . . When she was in the school room, our hours did not suit and I could very seldom have her to walk with me, but then on Sundays she was mine and we always walked together . . . yesterday when the hour came round, I could not help telegraphing to her how I was thinking of her and our walks.' Her wish to marry Prince Alfred, Queen Victoria's second son, aroused parental unease on both sides. Relations between Russia and Britain were strained but the young couple had their way, and they married in the Great Chapel of the Winter Palace in January 1872. Maria Alexandrovna found it difficult to settle at the British Court and only came into her own when her husband became Duke of Saxe-Coburg-Gotha.

(*Below left*) Maria Alexandrovna with her eldest child Prince Alfred, taken in Russia in about 1875.
(*Below right*) Her daughters Marie (*standing*), the future Queen of Romania, and Victoria Melita, whose marriages would become a matter of concern in Russia (*see pages 12, 107 and 214*).

Grand Princess Olga Konstantinovna (*right, with her mother*) became engaged to King George I of the Hellenes early in 1867, when she was just fifteen years old. Their meeting in her parents' home was said to have been accidental but it seems likely that his sister, the Tsarevna Maria Feodorovna, had played some part in it; certainly she persuaded Olga's reluctant parents to give their consent to the marriage. 'Where in the world have you, little rogue, ever learned to intrigue so well,' her father, King Christian IX of Denmark, asked her, 'since you must have worked hard against your uncle and aunt, who were previously decided against a match of this kind.' Olga was married in the Winter Palace in October and left for Greece soon afterwards, still very much a child. She took her favourite dolls and toys, which comforted her when the whole experience became overwhelming. She settled well and in time became a popular Queen, but at heart she was always Russian.

Queen Olga of the Hellenes, taken in Vienna in the 1870s.

Queen Olga with her elder sons, Constantine, the heir to the Greek throne (*right, seated*), and George. Constantine was born in August 1868, before his mother had even reached her seventeenth birthday, and his name was chosen by the crowd who chanted it below the palace balcony on the night of his birth. It was a curious turn of events: the first Constantine in the imperial family, Grand Prince Konstantin Pavlovich, had been given the name by his grandmother Catherine the Great, enshrining her desire to raise him one day to the throne of Greece, then in Turkish hands. Now, almost a century later, one of her descendants, still bearing the name, was in line to inherit the Greek throne.

King George and Queen Olga in 1881. The King and Queen were regular visitors to Russia and to the King's native Denmark, where his sister Maria Feodorovna, Alexander III and their children could also be found, particularly in autumn. The two families were always close.

Grand Princess Vladimir, Maria Pavlovna, with her brother, Hereditary Grand Duke Friedrich Franz of Mecklenburg-Schwerin, in 1878. Maria Pavlovna also used her position as a married woman to assist her single brothers; despite a gentle, almost saintly character, Friedrich Franz stood in particular need of her help. He suffered from severe asthma and spasmodic attacks of an unsightly skin condition. Maria Feodorovna left a graphic description: 'he has a rather revolting illness, a <u>rash</u> all over his neck and ears, all mattering so that he wore a kind of cloak for a whole week when he couldn't show himself otherwise! How terrible for him, poor thing . . . almost wrong for him to marry.' But Maria Pavlovna was just as skilled a hand in having her own way, and she noticed a potential bride in seventeen-year-old Grand Princess Anastasia Mikhailovna. Her brother visited St Petersburg and was certainly attracted so she took the matter in hand, initiating discussions with Anastasia's mother. 'You can imagine how agitated I was,' Maria Pavlovna told their father, 'because on this hangs the whole future life of my brother and also the welfare of our beloved Mecklenburg.'

Anastasia Mikhailovna in 1879, bearing out Maria Feodorovna's description of her on her wedding day: 'so sweet, as pretty as a rose, beautiful as a fairy'. Typically, the Tsarevna went on to give a vicious depiction of the bridegroom: 'like someone risen from the dead or someone they had forgotten to bury'. But Anastasia did come to love him; he was, by all accounts, a very lovable person – 'the dearest man on earth,' according to the Princess of Pless. It was with Mecklenburg-Schwerin itself that the problems arose. Before her wedding Anastasia made conscientious efforts to find out about the Grand Duchy but she found it impossible to settle. She hated the place and its people came to feel the same for her; before long, she and Friedrich Franz could only find happiness as a couple far from the country he was born to rule.

Anastasia's brother, Grand Prince Alexander Mikhailovich, with Grand Princess Ksenia Alexandrovna. This first marriage between members of the Romanov family was possible only because the couple were first cousins once removed.

Meeting among a group of youngsters who played and grew up together in the 1880s, they began as friends – though Alexander was almost nine years older than his future bride – and their feelings intensified as Ksenia reached her mid-teens. It was an attraction her parents, Alexander III and Maria Feodorovna, were not inclined to trust, partly because Ksenia was so young and partly because they were unsure of Alexander's character. But persistence paid off, and an engagement was finally agreed to in January 1894, after Grand Prince Mikhail Nikolaievich had intervened on his son's behalf. Even then, matters did not proceed smoothly; the Tsaritsa complained bitterly of Alexander's arrogance and rudeness, while he was equally bitter about the time that elapsed between the engagement and the wedding. The ceremony took place at Peterhof on 25 July/6 August 1894.

Alexander and Ksenia with their first child, Princess Irina Alexandrovna, in about 1896. Though there would be six more children, all of them boys, the romantic attraction between the couple did not last. The Grand Prince was dissatisfied with the course of events in Russia and became frustrated with Court life. After about twelve years of marriage he and Ksenia began to spend prolonged periods outside Russia. Each welcomed the attentions of a lover – with the tacit understanding of the other. For Alexander, it was a woman identified only as 'Maria Ivanovna'; for Ksenia, an Englishman named Fane, who was still corresponding with her as late as the First World War. Nevertheless she and Alexander remained married in name and on reasonable terms, and they are buried together.

Grand Princess Elena Vladimirovna and her fiancé, Prince Max of Baden. Prince Max was a grandson of Maria Nikolaevna, Duchess of Leuchtenberg. He was attractive and wealthy and there was no shortage of royal mothers with plans for his future. In 1898 it seemed that Grand Princess Vladimir had won when Max became engaged to her daughter Elena. The announcements were made and the photographs taken, but then he changed his mind. The Vladimirs were furious, and gossip about Maria Pavlovna's desperate attempts to marry off her daughter spread and grew. In 1900 Elena's name was linked to the recently widowed King of Bulgaria. That same year Prince Nicholas of Greece, Queen Olga's third son, proposed, but Maria Pavlovna rebuked Elena for encouraging a man with neither prospects nor fortune. Her eyes were set on Albert, the future King of the Belgians, but her attempts to bring him to Russia fell through when he announced his engagement to a Bavarian princess.

In June 1902 Maria Pavlovna accepted defeat and allowed her daughter to accept Prince Nicholas of Greece (*left, with Elena*). His aunt, Maria Feodorovna, had misgivings: 'Their upbringing and their ways of looking at things are so different and divergent. A great deal of patience will be demanded on both sides. . . . it is true that she has a very brusque and arrogant tone that can shock people.' But Queen Olga, standing apart from the old rivalry that always set the two Marias on different sides, was more hopeful about the match, and in the event she was right. The grand manner instilled in Elena by her mother would always cause problems in the family but between themselves Nicholas and Elena were happy and their marriage endured.

Grand Princess Olga Alexandrovna and Duke Peter of Oldenburg at the time of their engagement in the spring of 1901. As an elderly woman, recalling the distant past from her exile in Canada, Olga described her first marriage as an empty sham. She felt she had been tricked into accepting Duke Peter's proposal and her biographer, Ian Vorres, concluded that her mother must have contrived the arrangement to keep her daughter at hand. It was not the case. Contemporary documents show that Maria Feodorovna was both amazed and bemused by what Olga had agreed to. It was an unlikely match: Peter was thirty-two years old to Olga's eighteen and as effete and sickly as she was robust and energetic. But she did accept him and in the early years he, at least, was very much in love. 'My Dearest, sweet Olga . . . I miss you and our house seems dead without you. I came into your room, thinking about the time we spent here together and I felt tears in my eyes.' 'You make me happy because I know you are happy. I am hugging you with love': the cold, disinterested man of popular report would not have voiced sentiments like these. Perhaps sentiment was simply not enough. For whatever reason, the marriage foundered and Olga, looking back from the perspective of a happy second marriage, could only associate it with failure.

Another engagement viewed through the distorting glass of memory was that of Maria Pavlovna the younger (*in white*) and Prince Vilhelm of Sweden, arranged by Maria's aunt and guardian, Elizaveta Feodorovna (*on the left*) in 1907. Maria would later blame Elizaveta for 'her haste to have me married, and the complete absence of any thought as to the sentimental side of such a compact', while admitting that she herself had enjoyed the attention at the time. 'She was full of life and very jolly,' another aunt, Grand Princess Maria Georgievna, said of her niece, 'but inclined to be self-willed and selfish, and rather difficult to deal with.' Unspoken in Maria Pavlovna's memoirs was her own desire to escape the disciplines of childhood: 'Then we will be able to travel together,' she wrote to Vilhelm during their engagement, 'and to live just as we wish and to suit ourselves. I'm looking forward to a wonderful life – a life full of love and happiness, just as you described to me in your last letters.'

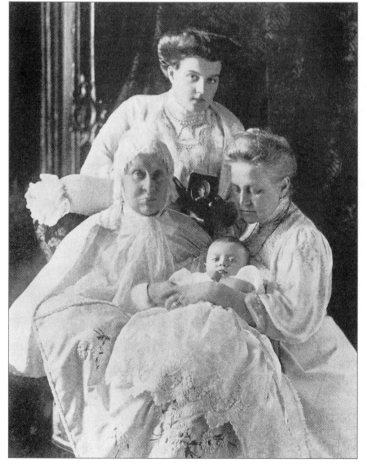

Five generations, with Maria Pavlovna the younger at the back, holding a photograph of her dead mother Alexandra, Grand Princess Pavel. Her grandmother Queen Olga of the Hellenes is on the right, her great-grandmother Alexandra Iosifovna, Grand Princess Konstantin, is on the left, and the baby is her son, Prince Lennart of Sweden, born in Stockholm on 8 May 1909. The happiness Maria anticipated in Sweden was not to be. As a serving naval officer, Vilhelm's life was subject to as many constraints as her own had been, and the Swedish Court too had its rules. Maria was frustrated and lonely, and became so ill that in 1913 her own family took her back to Russia and opened negotiations for a divorce. She abandoned her son, who remained with his father.

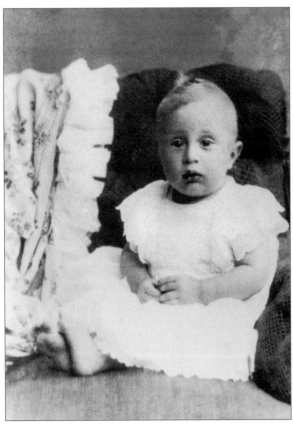

In May 1911 Princess Tatiana Konstantinovna became engaged to Prince Konstantin Bagration-Mukhransky. This was a sign of the changing times; with so many younger members of the family reaching marriageable age, there was little chance that partners of equal birth would be found for them all. Besides, most wanted to stay in Russia. So Nicholas II gave permission for Tatiana's marriage, and in August 1911 he formalised the new position in law by limiting the ruling on equal birth to the Grand Princes and Grand Princesses, the children and grandchildren of the Tsar in the male line. Older members of the family watched with misgivings: 'Did you hear that Uncle Kostia's daughter Tatiana is engaged to a Caucasian prince Bagration?' Grand Princess Maria Alexandrovna asked her daughter. 'The first morganatic female marriage in our family. She was simply dying and dwindling away on account of this morganatic love and now it has been sanctioned. A dangerous beginning in our family and the opening of a new social era.' The couple married at Pavlovsk on 24 August/6 September.

Prince Teymuraz Bagration-Mukhransky, born at Pavlovsk in the summer of 1912.

Princess Tatiana with her son.

Prince Teymuraz and his sister Princess Nathalie, who was born in Yalta in the spring of 1914.

The children's uncle, Prince Konstantin Konstantinovich, was so moved by the happiness his brother Ioann and sister Tatiana had found in their separate marriages that he too was keen to settle down. Maria Alexandrovna had noticed him in February 1911, with her granddaughter Princess Elisabeta of Romania in mind, but she feared that he was hoping for one of the Tsar's daughters. That autumn, however, she heard from his mother that he was keen to meet Elisabeta. She told Elisabeta's mother, 'The young Kostia is seized now with terror that she will be snatched away, as he says, before he has even made her acquaintance. The young man seems really quite nice, is much liked in his regiment and they have really been very well brought up. This one is full of life and they always have a pleasant existence at home, full of interests without any pedanterie. . . . If you have nothing against this youth coming on a passing visit, will you telegraph to me.' But the request was refused, apparently on political grounds, because Prince Ioann was married to a Serbian princess. Konstantin never did find the marriage he longed for.

Princess Irina Alexandrovna, only daughter of Grand Prince Alexander Mikhailovich, and Prince Felix Yusupov. Irina was the second family member to benefit from the relaxation in the marriage law. Prince Felix Yusupov, Count Sumarakov-Elston, was the only surviving son of one of Russia's richest couples – richer than the Tsars, it was said – but he was not a royal prince. Irina accepted his proposal early in 1913 and her parents agreed in principle, though no announcement was made. There were very grave doubts in the family because Felix had a bad reputation. They delayed the announcement to gain time and to make their own assessment of his character.

In the spring a second prospective husband came forward. Grand Prince Dmitri Pavlovich (*right*) told Felix that he loved Irina and intended to propose marriage. He proceeded to take every opportunity to spend time with her, encouraged, so Felix's mother believed, by Irina's grandmother Maria Feodorovna. Zinaida Yusupova discussed the situation with Irina's mother and told her son on 28 May/10 June, 'My dear boy. . . . Her mother does not deny that the grandmother is for Dmitry. But she says that she herself would have nothing against [you] if Irina will hear of no one else.' And so it proved to be. Irina's decision was already made, and in September the engagement was announced. The couple married in the Anichkov Palace in St Petersburg, the home of Irina's grandmother.

One of the first to rebel was Nikolai Konstantinovich (*above, with his mother Alexandra Iosifovna and sister Vera in about 1870*). Ignoring his mother's attempts to find him a suitable bride, Nikolai lavished his fortune on his mistress and his art collection. By 1874 he was stealing from the family: when this emerged he was declared insane, stripped of his rank and placed under supervision – but wherever he was taken, trouble followed. In 1874 and in 1876 a woman who should not even have come near him became pregnant by him; in 1878, in Orenburg, he married another woman in secret, and all the time he preached revolution. Officially he ceased to exist and, in the summer of 1881, Alexander III sent him into exile in Tashkent. In 1895, though still living with his wife, he bought a sixteen-year-old Cossack girl and started a family with her. In 1900 he contracted a bigamous marriage with a schoolgirl which was quickly annulled. Visiting him in 1904, his sister Olga said, 'he has completely lost any moral sense of what can be done and what can be demanded'. But there was another side to Nikolai. He took a serious interest in Central Asia, organising scientific expeditions and publishing his findings. In Tashkent he launched irrigation schemes and other beneficial projects. He welcomed the Revolution and, when he died of pulmonary disease in April 1918, local Bolsheviks arranged a grand funeral for him in Tashkent Cathedral.

Grand Prince Mikhail Mikhailovich came of age desperate to marry. He proposed to Princess Irène of Hesse in 1886 and Princess Louise of Wales in 1887, each time thinking himself deeply in love. Both refused. Later in 1887 he fell for Countess Ignatiev, a government minister's daughter. She accepted him but, after prolonged discussions, the Tsar refused to allow the marriage. In misery Mikhail fled for Europe where he fell in love with Sophie, Countess Merenberg (*right*), and married her before anyone could stop him. For this he was stripped of his rank and exiled. The photograph shows him with Sophie and their daughters Anastasia (*right*) and Nadejda in about 1898.

Four years after his first wife's death, Grand Prince Pavel started an affair with Olga von Pistolkors, the wife of his brother's aide-de-camp. When she gave birth to a son – his child – and the Tsar refused to grant von Pistolkors a divorce unless Pavel promised not to marry Olga, Pavel gave his word intending to break it. He fled from Russia, abandoning his legitimate children, and was married in Italy. For this he was banished and the children were placed under the guardianship of their uncle Sergei. Pavel became father to a second family; (*above*), with Vladimir, Irina (*standing*), Natalia and their mother, taken in 1916.

In 1896, at the coronation of Nicholas II, Grand Prince Kirill Vladimirovich fell in love with his cousin Victoria Melita, second daughter of Grand Princess Maria Alexandrovna. The fact that she was his first cousin would have been enough to confound any marriage plan but there was worse: she was married already to Grand Duke Ernst Ludwig of Hesse. But the Hesse marriage was under strain and it ended in divorce in 1901; according to Kirill, Victoria Melita took this step because she loved him. Over the next few years they lived together when they could, though Kirill's requests for permission to marry were regularly refused. Their behaviour caused much disquiet in the family and Kirill's parents did their utmost to end the relationship. His mother even urged him to keep Victoria Melita as his mistress and find some other princess to marry, for the sake of his position. In the autumn of 1905 the couple married in secret in Bavaria. When Kirill turned up in Russia expecting forgiveness, the Tsar stripped him of his rank and revenues and ordered him into exile.

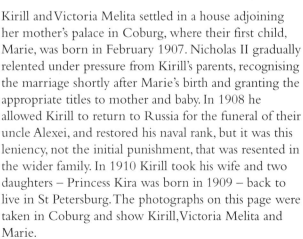

Kirill and Victoria Melita settled in a house adjoining her mother's palace in Coburg, where their first child, Marie, was born in February 1907. Nicholas II gradually relented under pressure from Kirill's parents, recognising the marriage shortly after Marie's birth and granting the appropriate titles to mother and baby. In 1908 he allowed Kirill to return to Russia for the funeral of their uncle Alexei, and restored his naval rank, but it was this leniency, not the initial punishment, that was resented in the wider family. In 1910 Kirill took his wife and two daughters – Princess Kira was born in 1909 – back to live in St Petersburg. The photographs on this page were taken in Coburg and show Kirill, Victoria Melita and Marie.

Neither of Kirill's brothers was willing to play by the rules. Boris never married and became a notorious playboy. In the summer of 1901 Grand Prince Andrei Vladimirovich (*left*) was introduced by his elder brothers to Mathilde Kschessinskaya. She described the moment: 'He was exceptionally good-looking and also very shy, which did not spoil things at all – quite the reverse! During dinner he accidentally knocked over a glass of red wine whose contents spilled on my dress. Far from being angry, I saw in this a happy omen . . . For from that moment my heart was filled with an emotion which I had not felt for a long time.' Since Nicholas II's accession and marriage, Mathilde had lived under the protection of his cousin, Grand Prince Sergei Mikhailovich. Society believed they were lovers, but her memoirs speak only of affection and friendship. Describing the birth of her son in the summer of 1902, at the dacha Sergei had bought for her, she wrote that he 'knew for certain that he was not the father of the child, but he loved me and . . . forgave me everything'.

Mathilde with her son Vladimir, known as 'Vova'. The relationship between Andrei and Mathilde continued, much to the annoyance of Grand Princess Vladimir. Sergei Mikhailovich also remained very much part of Mathilde's life.

For Nicholas II, the hardest defection of all was the runaway marriage of his brother Grand Prince Mikhail Alexandrovich (*right, taken in Denmark*). Mikhail was heir to the throne from 1899 until 1904, and the frail health of the Tsesarevich Alexei meant that at any moment the cup might pass to him again. No marriage was more vital to the continuation of the dynasty; unfortunately, Mikhail fell in love too easily. In 1902 it was Victoria Melita's younger sister Beatrice who caught his affections as he did hers. They corresponded, but in 1903, when the subject of marriage was raised, the Tsar told his brother that it could not be as Beatrice was his first cousin. Mikhail's attempts to end the relationship met with horrified protests from Beatrice's family and the argument lasted until 1905, but by this time he was in love again. The girl was a lady-in-waiting, Alexandra Kossikovskaya; in 1906 Mikhail asked permission to marry her. His brother refused and their mother had the lady-in-waiting very swiftly removed. In the summer of 1907 Mikhail planned two attempts to marry her in secret, both of which were foiled.

Before the end of 1907 a third woman had come into Mikhail's life. Natalia Sheremetyevskaya was married to an officer in his regiment, Vladimir Wulfert – her second husband. For her, flirtation with Mikhail was just a game – could she catch the heart of the Tsar's brother? She could, and she did. The relationship became more serious when Wulfert discovered it. He was a violent man, so Mikhail was dispatched to another regiment but he would not abandon Natalia and their affair became a constant nightmare for the Court. In July 1910 Natalia gave birth to Mikhail's son. In the autumn of 1912, with the Tsesarevich at the point of death, Mikhail broke his promise to his brother and married her secretly in Vienna. He was quite blatant about his reasons: 'I . . . might never have decided on this step, were it not for little Alexei's illness and the thought that as Heir I could be separated from Nathalie, but now that can no longer happen.' It was the cruellest reason he could have chosen. Nicholas exiled him: here, Mikhail, Natalia and their son George are pictured at Knebworth in England.

Grand Princesses Olga (*sitting*) and Tatiana Nikolaevna in the spring of 1914. Society was intrigued by the marriage prospects of the Tsar's elder daughters: would it be Grand Prince Dmitri Pavlovich? Prince Konstantin Konstantinovich? Prince Alexander of Serbia? In July 1914 the imperial family went to Romania to introduce Olga to Prince Carol of Romania but she was not impressed; for Princesses too, first love was likely to strike closer to home. For a few months at the end of 1913 Olga nursed an innocent passion for a junior officer on the imperial yacht *Shtandart*. His name was Pavel Voronov and the photograph below shows him and Olga together on the left, with Tatiana, Anastasia and another officer. Voronov danced with Olga in October 1913 and from that day her diary is filled with sightings of 'S', as she called him, and misery when he was not around. It seems he shared the feeling, but it was bound to end. In December came the announcement of Voronov's engagement to one of the ladies-in-waiting: 'God grant him good fortune, my beloved,' Olga wrote. 'It's sad, distressing.' Privately she continued to think of him for some time.

7

Family Ties

Before the reign of Peter the Great, in the seventeenth century, the Tsars married only Russian girls. Their daughters were rarely allowed to marry at all, for fear that a powerful husband or son might one day become a threat to the throne. They lived out their days in the terem, an enclosed, protected world of women and children, weaving, embroidering and waiting. Many took the veil. But by the nineteenth century the imperial family had become thoroughly integrated into the wider family of European royalty: these ties often played their part in the political direction the Tsars chose to follow. The Romanovs may still have seen themselves as a group apart and there were still differences in power, wealth and religious practice which other princes sometimes resented, but in reality they were all one family. This change really began with the daughters of Tsar Paul. He had six; four of whom, Grand Princesses Elena, Maria, Ekaterina and Anna, survived to marry foreign princes and to have children of their own. Through them, and through later marriages, the imperial family was able to boast a rich network of royal cousins – and to this day, many European monarchs and princes, reigning and non-reigning, have at least one line of Romanov ancestry.

The young Queen Wilhelmina of the Netherlands was a granddaughter of Grand Princess Anna Pavlovna. She married Duke Heinrich of Mecklenburg-Schwerin, a great-grandson of Elena Pavlovna, so their descendants have two lines of Romanov ancestry – a fact echoed in the names of Wilhelmina's granddaughter Queen Beatrix's sons, Willem-Alexander and Constantijn. Wilhelmina was drawn into the most imaginative political initiative of Nicholas II's reign, now all but forgotten. In 1898 the Tsar published his 'Peace Rescript', an appeal for arms reduction by international agreement: ultimately for an end to war. 'Here at last we have a monarch who has an eye to see the cancer which is eating into the heart of the modern state,' wrote the journalist W.T. Stead, and two conferences were convened at The Hague, in 1899 and 1907. Wilhelmina was Queen of the host country, but she feared the conferences would lead nowhere: 'I had little hope that conventions agreed at peace conferences would be observed in the case of a serious conflict.' It was a sad irony that the Tsar who began his reign with a sincere drive for peace should have ended in such violence.

King Willem III of the Netherlands, Wilhelmina's father, was the eldest son of Anna Pavlovna and Wilhelmina was the only child of his late second marriage to Princess Emma of Waldeck-Pyrmont. His first wife, Sophie of Württemberg, was also a Romanov descendant, the younger daughter of Grand Princess Ekaterina Pavlovna. The marriage was unhappy and the couple's three sons all died before their father.

King Willem's only sister Sophia (*centre*) married
her cousin Grand Duke Carl Alexander of Saxe-
Weimar (*seated, right*), the only surviving son of
Grand Princess Maria Pavlovna. This group,
taken in 1889, shows the couple with their
children; Hereditary Grand Duke Carl August
(*standing, right*) with his wife Pauline and sons
Wilhelm Ernst (*left, with his mother*) and Bernhard
(*front*); Princess Marie (*front left*) with her husband
Heinrich VII Reuss (*centre back*); Princess
Elisabeth (*front right*) with her husband Duke
Johann Albrecht of Mecklenburg-Schwerin (*in
uniform*). Duke Johann Albrecht was a great-
grandson of Grand Princess Elena Pavlovna.

Grand Duke Carl Alexander had two sisters. In
1829 the younger, Princess Augusta of Saxe-
Weimar (*right*), married Prince Wilhelm of
Prussia, Tsar Nicholas I's brother-in-law.
Wilhelm succeeded his brother as King of
Prussia and in 1871 became the first German
Kaiser. Through Augusta the later German
Kaisers, Friedrich III and Wilhelm II, and their
children, were descendants of Tsar Paul. Augusta
and Wilhelm's only daughter, Luise, became
Grand Duchess of Baden.

Grand Princes Nikolai (*left*) and Mikhail Mikhailovich, on a visit to Baden in 1876. Their mother Grand Princess Olga Feodorovna, born Princess Cäcilie of Baden, was the second of three Romanov connections with the Baden family. The first was the marriage of her brother Friedrich to Princess Luise of Prussia. Then in 1863 her brother Wilhelm married Princess Maria of Leuchtenberg, the elder daughter of Nicholas I's daughter Maria Nikolaevna. There was nearly a fourth connection when Grand Prince Nikolai Mikhailovich fell in love with his cousin Viktoria of Baden, the only daughter of Friedrich and Luise, but they were not allowed to marry. Viktoria went on to become Queen of Sweden, while Nikolai remained single.

Maria of Leuchtenberg, Princess Wilhelm of Baden, pictured with her grandchildren in 1907. Princess Marie Alexandra (*standing*) and Prince Berthold were the children of Prince Max of Baden. Two years after breaking off his engagement to Grand Princess Elena Pavlovna, Max married Princess Marie Louise of Cumberland. In the final weeks of the First World War he became Chancellor of Germany and it fell to him to sign the request for an armistice and the abdication of the Kaiser.

Grand Prince Mikhail Nikolaevich in 1899 with his daughter Grand Princess Anastasia Mikhailovna, Grand Duchess of Mecklenburg-Schwerin (*looking down*), her daughter Alexandrine, Princess Christian of Denmark, and Alexandrine's infant son Prince Frederik of Denmark. The Mecklenburg-Schwerin connection was a long one. Grand Princess Elena Pavlovna married the Hereditary Grand Duke at the end of the eighteenth century and died young, leaving him with two children. The elder, Paul Friedrich, became Grand Duke in his turn and was the grandfather of Anastasia's husband Friedrich Franz III – also of Grand Princess Vladimir and of their younger brothers Heinrich and Johann Albrecht (*see pages 112 and 113*). The photograph below shows Alexandrine (*centre*) with her children Grand Duke Friedrich Franz IV (*right*), Alexandrine (*left*) and Cecilie. The young man in the window is Alexandrine's husband Prince Christian of Denmark and the children are their sons Frederik and Knud. In 1947 Prince Frederik became King of Denmark.

Grand Princess Maria Alexandrovna, Duchess of Saxe-Coburg, with her daughters Beatrice, Victoria Melita and Alexandra. Beatrice, in the light dress, was the princess whose doomed love for Grand Prince Mikhail Alexandrovich, Nicholas II's brother, caused lasting bitterness between the two families.

A gathering of cousins on the lawns at Schloss Callenberg in Coburg in the early 1900s. The ladies are, from the left, Victoria Adelheid, Duchess of Saxe-Coburg, Marie, Crown Princess of Romania and her sister Victoria Melita; the men are Grand Prince Kirill, Prince Leopold of Battenberg and Charles Edward, Duke of Saxe-Coburg. The two couples in the picture, Kirill and Victoria Melita and the Duke and Duchess of Saxe-Coburg were married within a few days of each other in October 1905.

Maria Alexandrovna's cousin, Vera Konstantinovna, with her husband Prince Wilhelm Eugen of Württemberg. Vera's marriage to Wilhelm Eugen, in May 1874, enabled her to stay in Stuttgart with her aunt Queen Olga. But the marriage itself was tragically short-lived. The first child was a son, who died when he was seven months old. In 1876 Vera gave birth to twin girls, Princesses Elsa and Olga, but Wilhelm Eugen died before their first birthday. Vera remained in Stuttgart. The Queen loved her as a daughter and when she began writing her memoirs, in 1881, she dedicated them to the twins as if they were her grandchildren: 'Dear Children!,' she wrote, 'One day, perhaps, when you are grown up, you may want to know what your Grandmama's childhood was like in that distant land that was also the home of your mother, and no one from there who lived with me will be alive any longer to tell you . . .'

Grand Princess Vera with her family in about 1908/9. The twins married brothers Albrecht and Maximilian of Schaumburg-Lippe. Maximilian died in 1904. The photo shows Vera in the centre, between Elsa and her husband Albrecht. Their children are Max, sitting cross-legged in front, Franz Josef, between his father and grandmother, Alexander sitting on the right, and Bathildis. Olga stands at the back and her two sons are Eugen (*right, standing*) and Albrecht (*left*).

A very young Nicholas II (*seated, centre*) with his English cousins Prince George, later King George V (*left*), and Prince Albert Victor of Wales, photographed on a visit to Denmark in about 1871. The Danish connection, dating back to the engagement of Princess Dagmar (Maria Feodorovna) and the Tsesarevich Nikolai in 1864, was very influential, drawing together Danish, Russian, English and Greek cousins in regular autumn reunions.

The families at Bernstorff in 1871: (*from the top*) Maria Feodorovna holding her son, Georgi Alexandrovich; (*in front of her*) her sister, Princess Thyra; Alexandra, Princess of Wales, holding her daughter Princess Maud; (*behind*) Princess Victoria of Wales; Queen Louise of Denmark. (*On the steps in front*) Crown Prince Frederik of Denmark; Prince Albert Victor of Wales; (*behind, in white*) Grand Prince Nicholas Alexandrovich (Nicholas II); Prince George of Wales (George V); Princess Louise of Wales; Crown Princess Louise of Denmark holding her son, Prince Christian.

The families in 1884, or thereabouts: (*standing*) King George I of the Hellenes; the Princess of Wales; Crown Prince Frederik; Prince Waldemar of Denmark; Prince George of Greece. (*In front*) Grand Prince Mikhail Alexandrovich; Grand Princess Ksenia; their mother Maria Feodorovna holding Grand Princess Olga; Princess Louise of Denmark (daughter of the Crown Prince).

Alexander III in Denmark in the late 1880s with his sons Nicholas (*left*) and Georgi (*right*) and his nephew Crown Prince Constantine, the eldest son of Grand Princess Olga Konstantinovna, Queen of the Hellenes. Alexander III liked Denmark; holidays there gave him the opportunity to put on civilian clothes and break away from the oppressive security that surrounded him in Russia. The riotous, slapstick humour of the Danish royal family appealed to him too, and he joined in with relish.

Also photographed in the late 1880s, possibly during the same holiday, the sisters Maria Feodorovna (*centre*) and Alexandra, Princess of Wales, one with her oldest child and one with her youngest – Prince Albert Victor of Wales and Grand Princess Olga Alexandrovna.

A game of cards: (*from the left*) Princess Louise of Wales; Crown Prince Constantine of Greece; the Tsesarevich Nicholas; Prince George of Greece and Prince Albert Victor of Wales, with Grand Prince Georgi Alexandrovich watching from the wall.

The Tsesarevich Nicholas and Prince George of Greece amusing some of the younger members of the family party in about 1890. (*From the left*) Princess Alexandra of Cumberland, Nicholas holding Prince Christopher of Greece, George holding Prince Ernst August of Cumberland, Prince Christian, Prince Georg Wilhelm and Princess Olga of Cumberland. The Cumberlands were the children of Princess Thyra of Denmark, Maria Feodorovna's younger sister, and her husband Ernst August, Duke of Cumberland. The Duke was heir to the throne of Hanover, which had been seized by Prussia in the 1860s. They lived for the most part in Austria, but shared the Danish reunions. Prince Christopher was Prince George's little brother, born at Pavlovsk, his mother's childhood home, in the summer of 1888.

The cousins who shared the Danish autumns with their grandparents, King Christian IX and Queen Louise, formed many close friendships. This photograph of Nicholas as Tsar, with his cousin Princess Victoria of Wales, was taken in Denmark in 1901. As teenagers, in the autumn of 1883, Nicholas and Victoria had shared a brief, cheerful flirtation, recorded from day to day in Nicholas's diary: 'My evening game with Victoria is that she hides and I seek. When I find her too soon, she gets cross and starts chasing me. If she catches me she tries to knock me down. . . . In the evening I tried to be alone with her and kiss her: she is so lovely. . . . The more Victoria torments and teases her prey, the more the prey loves her. This prey is ME.' When they corresponded in later years, she was always 'Toria', her nickname in the family, while he was 'darling Old Nick'.

Nicholas owed a special debt to Prince George of Greece, pictured with him above. In Otsu in Japan in 1891 George saved his cousin's life by parrying a sabre blow from a would-be assassin.

George's sister Marie (*right*) became a close friend of Nicholas's sister Ksenia on her Danish and Russian holidays. In later life the two girls married brothers.

Prince Nicholas of Greece, who married Grand Princess Elena Vladimirovna, was another of the Greek cousins and brother to George and Marie. They had three daughters, pictured here with Elena in 1909: Olga, leaning against her mother's shoulder, Elisabeth (*right*) and Marina. In 1934 Marina married Prince George, Duke of Kent, the fourth son of her father's cousin King George V.

The 1901 visit to Denmark: Nicholas II out walking with his daughters Tatiana (*centre*) and Olga. The Tsar and Tsaritsa were on their way to France that autumn on a state visit. They enjoyed the family reunion in Denmark before travelling south, stopping on the way to leave their children with the Tsaritsa's sister Irène, Princess Heinrich of Prussia, at Kiel. The Russian children always attracted a lot of attention. Their nurse, Miss Eagar, described how King Edward VII made a special visit to the nursery to see them on his arrival in Copenhagen in 1901, with Queen Alexandra coming on ahead to check that everything was ready: 'She often said they were always so nicely dressed and kept.'

Alexandra Feodorovna on the same visit to Denmark with King Christian IX.

The English connection was also strong. In 1896 Nicholas II and Alexandra visited her grandmother Queen Victoria. This was taken at Balmoral and shows (*from the left, in front*) Arthur, Duke of Connaught and his daughter Patricia, the Princess of Wales; the Tsaritsa; Louise and Maud of Wales, the Tsar, Margaret of Connaught. (*Behind*) the Prince of Wales, the Duchess of Connaught, Helena Victoria of Schleswig Holstein; Carl of Denmark (Princess Maud's husband); Victoria of Wales.

The Hesse connection spanned four generations, with regular Russian visits to Darmstadt from the 1860s onwards. This was how Grand Prince Sergei Alexandrovich came to know his future wife, and at their wedding the last Tsar and Tsaritsa met. Above, on the steps of the Neues Palais in Darmstadt in October 1903, are the family guests from the wedding of Andreas of Greece and Alice of Battenberg, including many familiar faces (see Notes, p. 236).

Grand Princess Elizaveta Feodorovna (*left*) with her elder sister Victoria, Princess Louis of Battenberg, and Grand Prince Dmitri Pavlovich, taken by the Moscow photographer Karl Fisher, probably at Ilinskoe, the summer residence on the Moscow river which Grand Prince Sergei inherited from his mother. Victoria and Elizaveta were close from childhood and Victoria made a number of visits to Russia. Her younger son Lord Mountbatten amazed his Russian hosts on a much later visit by pointing out the rooms he had slept in as a child.

Their brother Grand Duke Ernst Ludwig (*left*) on a visit to Russia in 1908, taken in the Alexander Park at Tsarskoe Selo with Nicholas II and the little Tsesarevich Alexei (the photograph comes from Ernst Ludwig's own album).

Ernst Ludwig in his sister's room in the Alexander Palace with his nieces Olga (*left*) and Tatiana. The window corner of the Mauve Boudoir was always a favourite place for taking family snapshots, though the strong light coming in through the window almost always made for a poor exposure. In the Alexander Palace today a chair is placed in the window corner and a selection of copy prints recalls the many groups that were posed there.

In the autumn of 1910 the Tsar and his family made a long visit to Germany to enable the Tsaritsa to take a cure at the spa at Bad Nauheim, in the Grand Duchy of Hesse. They stayed in Schloss Friedburg, and the visit gave them ample opportunity to see the family and to explore the local area. Here, Alexei (in the white shirt) poses with his little cousins, Ernst Ludwig's sons Georg Donatus (*centre*) and Ludwig, on the hill leading up to the Adolfsturm in Friedburg. The woman on the left is the Hesse boys' Norland nurse Lilian Eadie; next to her is Alexei's nurse Maria Vishniakova, holding his coat and sailor cap; behind the children are the Hesse boys' nursery maid and Andrei Derevenko, the sailor who watched over Alexei. At a discreet distance the ever-present security men watch from the archway.

Grand Princesses Maria (*left*) and Anastasia on an outing to the Munzenberg on 5 September 1910, during the Friedburg visit. Both families were present: one of the elder Grand Princesses can be glimpsed in the background and the boy with the Eton collar and flat cap is probably Prince Louis of Battenberg, later Lord Mountbatten.

Alexei and the Hesse boys in the courtyard at Wolfsgarten, the Grand Duke of Hesse's country home.

At Schloss Friedburg: Alexei (*left*), Ludwig and Georg Donatus and two little Greek cousins, Margarita (*next to Alexei*) and Theodora, the daughters of Prince Andreas of Greece and Princess Alice of Battenberg, and the elder sisters of Prince Philip, Duke of Edinburgh.

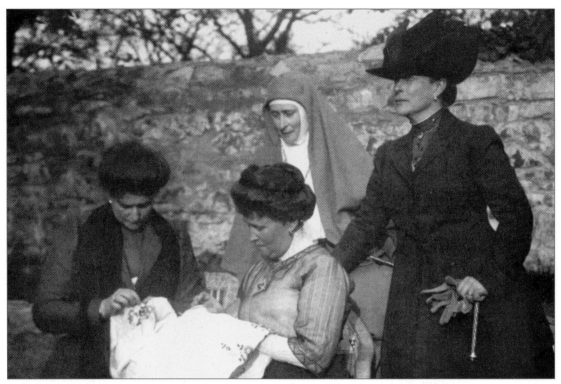

The Hesse sisters; (*from the left*) Alix, Irène, Elizaveta (in the nun's habit she adopted in 1910) and Victoria on 24 October 1910.

In 1912 Grand Duke Ernst Ludwig and his family visited the Crimea; he must have been a favourite uncle: here he carries Olga Nikolaevna . . .

. . . and here Tatiana. (*Above right*) Tatiana on board *Shtandart* with little Ludwig of Hesse, her cousin. (*Below*) Tatiana with her uncle (*right*) and an unidentified officer on *Shtandart*.

Grand Princess Elizaveta Feodorovna on a visit to her sister Irène, Princess Heinrich of Prussia, in July 1913, at Hemmelmark on the north German coast. In establishing her convent Elizaveta had made provision for the nuns to spend an annual holiday with their families. When this was questioned by the male clergy of the Holy Synod, to whom she had of necessity submitted her plans, she replied simply that it was intended 'for their refreshment'.

A picnic on the dunes at Hemmelmark for Ernst Ludwig, Elizaveta and their brother-in-law Prince Heinrich of Prussia.

8

The Family at Work

The Tsars were immensely hard-working men. An autocratic ruler may wield absolute power but he carries absolute responsibility too, and the work-load of the Tsars was crushing. At one moment the Tsar might find himself taking his country into war; at another, granting a divorce or a legal change-of-name for someone in a remote province of his empire. Society looked to him for amusement, the military for leadership, business and the arts for patronage and the distressed for help. The one thing Nicholas I, Alexander II, Alexander III and Nicholas II had in common, apart from the crown, was their reluctance to wear it. Even as children they guessed at its weight. But they were conscientious men who loved their country. The failure of Tsardom and generations of negative propaganda have tended to trivialise their lives and to obscure all that they tried to do for Russia.

But monarchy is also a family business. The Tsaritsas carried an daunting weight of public expectation – to produce and rear children, to support their husbands, to lead fashionable society and to champion a wide range of causes, primarily in the fields of education and the caring services. The uncles, aunts and cousins too were expected to play their part: at all times, but especially in times of crisis, family involvement was crucial.

Alexander II in his study: a Levitsky photograph with a painted background which accurately represents the real study in the Winter Palace where Alexander spent time as a child, where he worked throughout his adult life and where he died, in one of the curtained alcoves, his body shattered by a terrorist's bomb. A new plaque and a marble bust placed in the room in recent years recall the importance that once it had. A large part of any Tsar's working life was spent behind a desk, reading or hearing reports from his ministers, writing letters, studying government papers, receiving deputations and giving audiences.

This postcard commemorates a later anniversary of the most important single reform enacted in Alexander's reign, the emancipation of the serfs. The Manifesto was signed on 19 February 1861. This combination of photographic portraits and decorative artwork was typical at the end of the nineteenth and beginning of the twentieth centuries, when photographic illustration first appeared in magazines. The smaller portraits show the men who served in Alexander's reforming committee including, at top centre, his brother Grand Prince Konstantin Nikolaevich.

Nicholas I trained his younger sons to work as a
disciplined team, under the Tsar. Konstantin
Nikolaevich (*top left*) was prepared from childhood to
command the Russian navy. With his aunt Elena
Pavlovna he was active in creating the aid organisation
which became the Russian Red Cross; he also played a
political role – without him, the emancipation of the
serfs might never have happened. In 1862 he became
Alexander's Viceroy in Poland and this taught him a
harsh lesson about the dangers of reform. Konstantin
ended martial law and embarked on a programme of
liberalisation. But after years of repression the screw was
released too quickly and in 1863 his government
crumpled in the face of armed rebellion. Konstantin
remained a power at his brother's side, as Chairman of
the State Council. He was an active member of various
artistic and scientific societies.

Nikolai Nikolaevich, the second brother (*top right*),
was Military Governor of the district of St Petersburg,
General Inspector of Cavalry and an influential military
figure; he also served on the State Council. In
December 1862 the youngest brother, Mikhail
Nikolaevich (*right*), became Alexander's Viceroy in the
Caucasus, a post he was to hold for nineteen years.

Alexander III came to the throne on the day of his father's assassination and he wasted no time in removing the uncle whose liberal policies he blamed for what had happened. It was the consequence of years of political disagreement and personal animosity between the new Tsar and his uncle Konstantin. The important post of Chairman of the State Council went to Grand Prince Mikhail Nikolaevich, the only uncle whose services Alexander III retained. The reign was characterised by tightened security and increased control; later, some would see it as a golden age for the monarchy while others would blame Alexander III for starting the slide towards Revolution.

Like his father before him, Alexander III used his brothers to extend his reach. His relationship with Grand Prince Vladimir had always been coloured by a faint edge of resentment, brought into open rivalry by their wives. Nonetheless, on the day after their father's death he appointed Vladimir Military Governor of St Petersburg, a post that was previously held by their uncle Nikolai. Vladimir served on the State Council and chaired the official commission that supervised the building of a memorial church for Alexander II. In 1876 he took over the Presidency of the Academy of Arts on the death of the previous President, his aunt Maria, Duchess of Leuchtenberg; he was also a member of the Academy of Science.

Grand Prince Sergei Alexandrovich (*right*) commanded the prestigious Preobrajensky Regiment. In the spring of 1891 Alexander III appointed him Governor General of Moscow, a duty he accepted with profound regret: 'he was hoping to stay another year in the regiment,' his wife told her father. 'It makes one's hair stand on end when one thinks how much responsibility is placed on Serge.' History has judged the Grand Prince harshly for his rule in Moscow but even this story has another side. Alexander III's repressive policies were certainly enacted by the Grand Prince, particularly against the city's Jews, but even after years of Sergei's rule Moscow did not feel like a city under tyranny. The American traveller Burton Holmes, visiting in 1901, found a contented, modern city where the imperial family were able to move freely in the streets. He attended the Battle of Flowers, a high-spirited charity event presided over by Sergei and Elizaveta with only minimal policing. In 1900 and 1903 the Tsar and Tsaritsa attended the Easter services in the Kremlin and were able to stand unguarded in the worshipping crowds on Cathedral Square. In modern Russia even Sergei's reputation is undergoing a transformation.

To take over from his uncle Konstantin in command of the Russian navy, Alexander III trusted his brother Grand Prince Alexei Alexandrovich (*left*). Like Sergei, Alexei has been harshly judged by history but not, this time, for hard-line policies. Quite the opposite: the traditional view of Alexei is of a lazy, pleasure-loving incompetent responsible for the naval defeats of the Russo–Japanese War of 1904. It certainly is true that Alexei was quite different in temper and attitude from his uncle Konstantin but, as a serving officer of many years' standing when he took command, he knew and cared about the navy. The future Kaiser Wilhelm II was shown around the naval base at Kronstadt by Alexei in 1884 and reported home, 'Since he had taken over the naval administration with its heavy responsibility – although at first with great reluctance – he has become much more serious and grave. In my voyage to Kronstadt I had the opportunity to converse at some length with him, and in the course of our talk he touched lightly on the frightful conditions which he found when he took over; in the walk round Kronstadt also he proved to be well acquainted with the different localities.'

It was only in the last reign that the 'family firm' devolved on one man alone. One of Nicholas II's brothers died in infancy, the second was too ill to survive the northern climate and the third was too young, then too busy with his love-life. Nicholas was forced to rely on his uncles – Vladimir, Alexei and Sergei all remained in office for the first decade of the reign – but the relationship was never so straightforward as when the Tsar was the older man. The young Tsar was diffident: 'He is weighed down by his exalted rank,' his cousin Konstantin Konstantinovich wrote, soon after the accession. 'His modesty suffers from having to be everywhere and always the first.' The photograph illustrates both the depth of the workload that weighed on the Tsar, and Nicholas's characteristic attitude to it. In 1909 a new campaign uniform was proposed for the Russian infantry. It could not be introduced without the Tsar's approval and Nicholas would not approve it without trying it himself. In private he donned the proposed uniform of an ordinary soldier and made two long marches along the Crimean coast, carrying full packs and equipment.

Other members of the family continued to fill worthwhile positions. In 1889 Grand Prince Konstantin Konstantinovich became President of the Academy of Science. In 1899 Nicholas II appointed him head of Russia's military training institutions, a position he accepted with interest though he was sorry to give up command of his regiment. He did not expect the appointment: 'I think they make me out to be a man of the liberal tendency, almost a red, and that he [the Tsar] will come to the opinion that it is better not to appoint me to a post, where I would be responsible either for educating the people or bringing up the young.' The photograph shows the presentation of a new standard to the Alexander II Cadet School in about 1906; Konstantin appears to the left of the standard behind his sons Igor, Oleg and Konstantin.

The public expected and needed to see their rulers. Here, in 1901, Nicholas II rides across Palace Square in St Petersburg beside a carriage containing the two Tsaritsas, his mother and his wife, bound for a review on the Field of Mars. The photograph was taken by the Bulla agency; founded in the 1890s, it became responsible for an increasing number of official photographs of the Tsar's public appearances.

Here, at Livadia in the Crimea in the autumn of 1909, Nicholas meets representatives of the local zemstva – elected regional councils established in his grandfather's reign, with limited responsibilities in the fields of education, transport and health. General Spiridovich, who was responsible for the security of the imperial family, recalled that at this particular meeting one of the delegates was a known republican. The Tsar had prepared himself with information about the local area and talked at length with the delegates about local needs. The republican came away in tears, saying, 'He could not have been more gracious to us.'

In 1900 Nicholas II decided to revive a tradition of his family and spend Easter in Moscow. It was Peter the Great who founded the new city and capital of St Petersburg but Moscow remained the heart of the old Russia and of the Russian church. Since the defeat of Napoleon in 1812, there was a revival in feeling towards Moscow and all it represented, and each successive Tsar was more Russian in sympathy than the one before. This photograph, by the Bulla agency, shows Nicholas and Alexandra riding through the Kremlin on the 1900 visit.

A devout Christian, Nicholas was closely concerned with church affairs and, together with many other members of the imperial family, he attended the ceremonies that marked the canonisation of St Seraphim of Sarov, from 15 to 20 July 1903. In this photograph the saint's remains are carried past the Assumption Cathedral in Sarovsk; the pall bearers include the Tsar himself, at the front, and Grand Princes Sergei Alexandrovich and Nikolai Nikolaevich the younger. Devotion to St Seraphim was strong within the imperial family and the Tsaritsa believed that her attendance at the canonisation had enabled her to conceive a son: Alexei was born a year later.

In the summer of 1912 Russia celebrated the centenary of the battle of Borodino, a heroic stand against Napoleon which led ultimately – though not initially – to the Grand Army's retreat from Moscow. Here, Nicholas II, Alexandra and their elder daughters (the one in front is Olga) receive gifts of bread and salt – a traditional gesture of welcome – from peasants on their arrival in Moscow. Bulla's camera has missed the peasants, but captures the delight on the faces of the imperial family and members of their suite.

A year later and an even bigger celebration, the Tercentenary of 1913, which marked three hundred years of Romanov rule. The imperial family – including aunts, uncles and cousins – made a triumphal progress around the country, greeted by enthusiastic crowds, but this photograph was taken in the heart of the Kremlin. Much to the imperial couple's sorrow the Tsesarevich was unable to walk, as he was still recovering from his most serious haemophilic attack in the previous autumn. For the Borodino celebrations he had been well and had performed his first independent public engagement, but in 1913 he had to be carried by a soldier of the escort.

Meeting other heads of state was another important function. Here, in 1898, Alexandra rides through the park at Peterhof with the German Kaiserin Auguste Viktoria.

(*Right*) The Tsar and Tsaritsa arriving in Stockholm on 16 June 1909. The tall figure on the extreme right is the Swedish King Gustav V; to the right of the Tsaritsa in the background is his son Vilhelm, husband of Grand Princess Maria Pavlovna the younger.
(*Below*) The Tsar at Krasnoe Selo in 1901 with King Carol I of Romania, whose armies made a decisive intervention on the Russian side in the Turkish War of 1877–8, in the reign of Nicholas's grandfather. The figure behind them is Grand Prince Vladimir.

The Tsar (*left*) and Kaiser Wilhelm II on board the German imperial yacht *Hohenzollern* on 4 June 1909. The Kaiser was an inconvenient relative. Few of his cousins felt at ease with him, yet diplomacy required them to be friendly. On this occasion Nicholas sailed on a barge from *Shtandart* to the *Hohenzollern*, stayed half an hour, then left to await the return visit. A photograph was taken on board *Shtandart* of the Kaiser, the imperial couple and their children, with the large, expensive dolls Wilhelm had brought. Everyone looks awkward in it except the Kaiser; he is grinning broadly.

Most princes held honorary rank in foreign armies. When they travelled, they carried these uniforms with them as etiquette often required them to arrive in the uniform of their host country. Here, in 1913, the cousins Nicholas II (*left*) and George V are photographed in Berlin in their German uniforms. The occasion was the wedding of the Kaiser's only daughter, Viktoria Luise, to Prince Ernst August of Cumberland, which proved to be the last great meeting of European royalty before the First World War. It was also the last meeting between Nicholas and George.

Ladies of the Russian Court wore uniform of a different kind: the Court dress we have already seen in childish form on the little Grand Princesses. This costume was introduced by Nicholas I for all the ladies of the Court, with differences in colour and ornamentation to denote their differences in rank. There does not appear to be a representation of the Tsaritsa Maria Alexandrovna in Court dress. Her daughter-in-law Maria Feodorovna (*left*) excelled on great occasions. Pretty and vivacious, enjoying fine clothes and blessed with great charm of manner, she was made for the social role of empress and society loved her.

Alexandra Feodorovna, on the other hand, though she was no less attractive, disliked the spectacle and the superficiality of the social world. She looked beautiful, but she never looked comfortable, and the awareness that Court and society did not like her drove her further into herself.

Court ladies on parade for the coronation of Nicholas II in Moscow in May 1896. (*From the left, standing*) Grand Princess Vera Konstantinovna, Duchess of Württemberg; Grand Princess Anastasia Mikhailovna, Grand Duchess of Mecklenburg-Schwerin; Maria Pavlovna, Grand Princess Vladimir; Grand Princess Elena Vladimirovna (partially obscured by the Duchess of Connaught's feather); Elizaveta Mavrikievna, Grand Princess Konstantin Konstantinovich; Hélène, Princess Albert of Saxe-Altenburg. (*In front*) Duchess Elsa of Württemberg; Alexandra Iosifovna, Grand Princess Konstantin Nikolaevich; Louise Margaret, Duchess of Connaught. Russian Court dress is worn by all the ladies in the group except the Duchess of Connaught, representing Queen Victoria, and Duchess Elsa. Princess Albert of Saxe-Altenburg was Russian, having been born and brought up in St Petersburg as a granddaughter of Grand Prince Mikhail Pavlovich. Many would later describe the striking beauty of the older Grand Princess Konstantin on this occasion: 'exceedingly tall and still astonishingly upright for her age, her hair was snow white; clothed from head to foot in silver she wore a sparkling diadem like frosted sun rays . . . Having a too great wealth of pearls to wear them *all* round her neck, she had fixed half a dozen ropes at her waist with an enormous diamond pin; they hung down along her gown in a milky cascade. She was so pale and shining white that seen against the golden walls of the cathedral she seemed to be covered with hoar-frost.'

Nicholas II was always most at home in his military role: this photograph shows him (*second left*) riding with his staff.

At a troop review on the Field of Mars (to the left of the mounted officer with the sabre).

At a church parade at Krasnoe Selo: the Tsar is in the centre, facing the camera, beside Grand Prince Vladimir.

Alexandra Feodorovna rarely rode a horse, and was seldom photographed in uniform though she held rank in more than one regiment. These photographs are an exception. Taken on the same occasion in May 1903, they show her playing a full part in the Jubilee celebrations of the Guard Uhlans, in uniform (*on the right*) and (*above*) mounted, on the extreme left, looking back at the Tsar. 'She was a true soldier's daughter,' Sophie Buxhoeveden remembered, 'and enjoyed these expeditions, military pageants, and reviews, and camp life with bands playing, bugles sounding, and regiments marching.'

Grand Princess Olga Alexandrovna wearing the uniform of her regiment, the 12th Akhtyrsky Hussars.

In wartime it was traditional for royal ladies to involve themselves in relief work of some kind. These photographs come from a series showing the sklad – a collection, storage and distribution centre – established in the Grand Kremlin Palace by Grand Princess Elizaveta Feodorovna, in her capacity as wife to the Governor General. In the first photo (*above*) she is seated behind the desk receiving donations, beneath the vast canvas by Ilya Repin of Alexander III and his family which now hangs in Moscow's Tretyakov Gallery. In the second photo (*below left*) Elizaveta is the central figure behind the table, in the light hat, collecting up bandages.

The Grand Princess (*seated*) in the bandage store.

Grand Princess Elizaveta Mavrikievna (*centre right*) and her daughter Princess Tatiana Konstantinovna (*centre*) on 14/27 September 1910, at the raising of the cross of the Church of the Saviour on the Waters, erected by Grand Prince Konstantin and his sister Olga, Queen of the Hellenes, in memory of sailors lost in the Russo–Japanese War. The funds were raised by public subscription from all classes by a committee headed by Queen Olga, whose attachment to the Russian navy was profound, dating back to her father's service as Admiral-General. At the time of her marriage her uncle Alexander II gave her the honorary rank of Admiral – the only time this was ever conferred on a woman. The church was inaugurated on 31 July 1911 and its bronze panels listed the names of all naval casualties of the war as equals, making no distinction for rank or religion. The woman to the left of Princess Tatiana is Mme Baltazzi, Queen Olga's lady-in-waiting.

The idea of holding bazaars in support of charity, serving themselves and often selling items they had made, was one that Alexandra Feodorovna and her sister Elizaveta learned in childhood from their mother Princess Alice. This photograph comes from an album dedicated to the new palace at Livadia that Alexandra gave to their brother Ernst Ludwig as a Christmas present in 1911. It was captioned in her own hand, 'My bazar at Yalta.'

9

The Family at Play

The standard set by Nicholas I for his male descendants was a harsh one, with service to the state their first and only priority. But even the most dedicated soldier needs to relax, and the camera tells us a lot about the imperial family in their off-duty moments – about their hobbies, pleasures and particular talents. Throughout the nineteenth century the family boasted a number of very gifted artists. A little modest dabbling in sketching and watercolour painting was a normal part of the education of well-bred young ladies in the period, but some of the Grand Princesses showed talent well beyond the norm. Many princes were not taught at all, so it is striking to find that Alexander II, Nicholas II and several of the Grand Princes were excellent draughtsmen; recently published drawings by Nicholas's brother Grand Prince Georgi Alexandrovich show that he was exceptional. Then there was music; many members of the family played an instrument of some kind, and for a time in the late 1800s there was even a family orchestra good enough to satisfy its members, if no one else. Acting was popular in the family too, and, of course, photography.

The camera also recaptures the atmosphere of the various palaces that were home to the imperial family and their favourite holiday settings, and all the scenes and seasons of the Russian year.

Tsaritsa Maria Alexandrovna was a quiet woman, most at ease in the domestic circle. She collected small glass ornaments – an interest inherited by her son Alexander III – and was often photographed with some kind of handicraft. Here, in the mid-1860s, she is working on what appears to be a very long canvas work runner.

In this photograph, taken some ten years later, the Tsaritsa is knitting while her son Pavel (*left*) studies a photograph album and his brother Sergei reads. Knitting may seem a rather incongruous pastime for an empress – after all, there was no demand in the Winter Palace for comfy cardigans or woolly hats – but we are told that a much more imperious member of the family, Maria Alexandrovna's daughter-in-law Grand Princess Vladimir, liked to knit in the evening while her husband read to her. Knitted articles were often used in the nursery in the 1870s and by this time Maria Alexandrovna had an ever-growing flock of grandchildren. Shawls, blankets and other items would have been welcomed by her various charities, too, and they were much in demand in wartime.

Three generations on, Maria Alexandrovna's great-granddaughter Olga sits knitting in the window corner of her mother's Mauve Boudoir while the little Tsesarevich looks on. Olga's handiwork would almost certainly have been intended either as a family present or as an item for sale in one of her mother's charity bazaars. Baroness Buxhoeveden recalled that the Tsaritsa never allowed her daughters to be idle; when they were too old for toys, they were encouraged always to have a piece of knitting or sewing to work on. They also enjoyed drawing and painting, though they did not share their father's artistic gift.

The Tsaritsa herself, Alexandra Feodorovna, on board the yacht *Shtandart* with her husband, working on a piece of embroidery. Alexandra did some exceptionally fine needlework, particularly ecclesiastical embroidery. The Russian Orthodox Church in Darmstadt, her childhood home, still preserves some pieces created by her in the style of the Russian artist Victor Vasnetsov, her contemporary.

Grand Princess Olga Alexandrovna was the youngest child of an artistic family and excelled in drawing and painting from an early age. The children of Alexander III were taught well and, because drawing meant so much to Olga, and other lessons so little, she was allowed to draw while other subjects were being taught, to help her concentrate. She excelled in watercolour painting, particularly of flowers, scenes and still-life. During the First World War she began to have work published in postcard form to raise money for charity (see p. 200) and after the Revolution she was able to earn money by selling her paintings.

Princess Marina Petrovna was another gifted artist. Her brother remembered, 'While she was still a child Marina already showed a clear gift for drawing and later she studied painting with great enthusiasm, first with a teacher from the senior school in Yalta and then in St Petersburg under Professor Kordovsky. Orlov, the drawing-master from Yalta, also taught Nadja and me. He was an outstandingly good teacher and a charming man: all three of us owed him our thanks for awakening our love of drawing and painting. Gradually as Marina's gift developed she began to paint pictures that astonished her teacher, not only by their technical quality but also by their inspired composition. My father, who took so much interest in painting himself, was delighted by Marina's talent.'

Grand Princess Alexandra Iosifovna played the piano and had some compositions of her own made public: a cantata to the memory of her parents, for example, published in St Petersburg, and a piano duet published in Vienna and dedicated 'to my much-loved son Nicholas'. She married into one of the most musical households in Russia: her husband, Grand Prince Konstantin Nikolaevich studied the cello under Ivan Seifert and in 1873 became Chairman of the Imperial Musical Society. The Konstantinovich palaces, Pavlovsk and Strelna, were concert venues for the finest musicians in Europe. Johann Strauss played at both and composed a quadrille entitled 'The Strelna Terrace'. His 'Alexandra' waltz was dedicated to the Grand Princess.

Her son Grand Prince Konstantin Konstantinovich, also a talented musician with a particular interest in church music, playing for his sister Olga and cousin Sergei.

Konstantin Konstantinovich will always be remembered best for his writing. He wrote poetry from childhood and began to publish in 1886 under the initials 'KR'. His work was well received and Tchaikovsky and others wrote musical settings for his lyrics. He also wrote plays. Alexander III suggested a Russian translation of *Hamlet* and at the long-awaited performance, in the Hermitage Theatre in February 1900, Konstantin took the title role (*left*).

His final play, *The King of the Jews*, was performed in the autumn of 1913; the photographs below show him as Joseph of Arimathea, and his son Prince Konstantin as a Roman prefect. In the summer of 1914 the Grand Prince recited the 'Nunc Dimittis' from his play at a reception at Pavlovsk. Baroness Buxhoeveden was there with Nicholas II's elder daughters and recalled: 'It was a moving and admirable piece of poetry and its author, then already a sick man, with his fine features bearing the stamp of the many emotions of a sensitive spirit, his hair and beard streaked with grey, looked like an inspired patriarch taking leave of the world. . . . "It is like a farewell," Tatiana Nicolaievna whispered to me. I felt this too. It was the farewell to his work – the last legacy of a true poet.'

Konstantin Konstantinovich was a remarkable man with a remarkable gift, but acting was a pleasure most of the family shared. Here, in a performance of extracts from Pushkin's *Eugene Onegin* in the theatre at Tsarskoe Selo in 1890, a young Nicholas II takes the part of Onegin opposite his aunt Elizaveta Feodorovna, Grand Princess Sergei, as Tatiana Larina. Both Nicholas and Konstantin Konstantinovich took the name 'Tatiana' for their daughters from *Eugene Onegin*.

Even the children joined in – and not only the young Konstantinovichi. Prince Roman Petrovich described his first experiences of acting in one of the halls of Znamenka, his father's summer palace near Peterhof, with scenery and props designed by his father. The family were the audience. At one performance Roman, his sister Nadejda and a friend, all in mouse costumes, recited French poetry 'with great feeling . . . our appearance drew such applause from Vladimir Alexandrovich that after the curtain fell his voice boomed out for "the actors" to appear once again'. As the children grew older they began to perform walk-on or supporting roles in the Russian plays performed at the private theatre of Sergeievka, then the home of their aunt Stana in her first marriage to Duke Georg of Leuchtenberg. Here, the children are in costume for one of the Sergeievka plays: Roman is in the centre with his elder sister Marina on the right and Nadejda sitting at his feet. The other girl is their cousin Elena of Leuchtenberg.

For the bicentenary of the city of St Petersburg in 1903 the imperial couple gave a ball in the Winter Palace, the like of which had never been seen. Guests were asked to wear the costume of the mid-seventeenth century – the reign of Tsar Alexei, the 'gentle Tsar' who was Nicholas II's favourite ancestor. Preparation of the costumes took months and they were kept secret, though the fashionable photographers of the city must have seen it all. A commemorative album was issued with photographs of all the guests, taken before the event. Grand Prince Mikhail Alexandrovich is shown wearing a diamond clip in his cap which belonged to the crown jewels and was lost on the night; despite an extensive search it was never found. Grand Prince Sergei and his wife's portraits were taken by the Moscow photographer Asikritov before they left for the capital. The photographs show (*top row, from the left, on this page and the next*) the Tsar and Tsaritsa; Grand Princess Elizaveta and Grand Prince Sergei; Grand Princes Mikhail Alexandrovich and Andrei Vladimirovich. (*Right*) Grand Prince Alexander Mikhailovich and Grand Princess Ksenia; Grand Princes Georgi Mikhailovich and Mikhail Nikolaevich, the sole representative of an earlier generation.

From the late 1880s amateur photography was a passion which the family shared, and outdoor groups of the period without at least one royal person clutching a box camera are rare. This photograph taken in Denmark in 1899 captures four royal amateurs at work: Alexandra Feodorovna stands just to the right of centre and there is a second lady, almost completely obscured, behind her. To the right, bending down over her viewfinder, is Maria Feodorovna and the figure behind her is probably Princess Victoria of Wales. Their victims include Nicholas II and his sister Olga, Aage, Axel, Erik and Margarethe of Denmark and Mikhail Alexandrovich; Xenia Alexandrovna and her husband have turned their backs to the cameras and the child in the centre is their son Prince Andrei.

On the lawns of the old Livadia palace in September 1909 are (*from the left*) Count Frederiks, an unknown Court lady, Mme Tiutcheva, Grand Princesses Maria, Anastasia and Olga, the Tsaritsa (camera at the ready), Grand Princess Tatiana, the Tsar and Admiral Nilov.

(*Right*) A very young photographer, the Tsesarevich Alexei, from a sequence of still photos taken in the Alexander Park in about 1906. They include the Tsaritsa holding the camera, Alexei running with it, his sisters in hot pursuit, and several portraits of the little boy clutching his prize.

(*Below*) Nicholas and Alexandra out walking, carrying the inevitable box camera.

The last Tsar found physical exercise and outdoor activities essential to his well-being. Hunting was a traditional pastime for men of his class and time. Pictured with him and Alexandra in this 1902 group are Grand Princes Nikolai Nikolaevich the younger (*standing, extreme left*), Vladimir (*sitting beside Alexandra*) and Mikhail Nikolaevich (*sitting, second from the right*).

Snow was a fact of the Russian winter and the family found many ways to enjoy it. Here, in the winter of 1907/8, Alexei shovels snow in the Alexander Park with his father.

The little Tsesarevich in a sleigh in the courtyard of the Alexander Palace. The part of the building behind the trees (for comparison with a more recent photo, see p. 226) housed the private rooms of the imperial family while the sleigh is parked closest to the guest wing, with the rooms of the Dowager Tsaritsa (Nicholas II's birthplace) and of Grand Princess Elizaveta Feodorovna.

(*Above left*) In the same winter the Tsar and Tsaritsa pose in the park with one of their dogs. Pets were important to the family; when they died, they were buried in the pet cemetery on the Children's Island, in the lake beside the Alexander Palace. The island was given its name in the reign of Nicholas I when it was set aside for his children with a playhouse and fort, similar to the ones enjoyed by Queen Victoria's children at Osborne.

(*Above right*) Anastasia dressed for the snow in 1910.

Alexei shovelling snow in 1910, apparently still wearing the same very beautifully decorated fur-lined coat and astrakhan cap as in the earlier photographs.

Summer, and the Tsar and his daughter Tatiana pull the oars while Olga and her mother look on, in a photograph almost certainly taken from the deck of the imperial yacht.

The yacht *Shtandart* was a floating palace, built for the family in Denmark in the 1890s. Here, Alexandra nurses the ship's cat, with Tatiana (*left*), Alexei and Olga.

Alexei on *Shtandart* in about 1908.

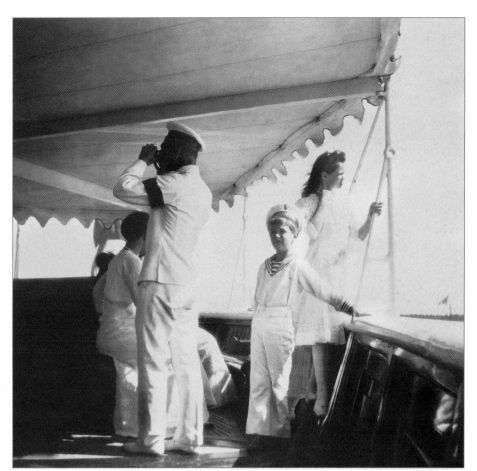

The yacht was in regular use by the family until the Revolution. In the photo on the right, taken in 1910 or 1911, the Tsar and Grand Princess Maria are watching something happening at sea; other shipping, perhaps, or a naval review or simply the passing coastline. The photos below are later, probably 1913, and show Alexandra with Maria and Alexei with his father.

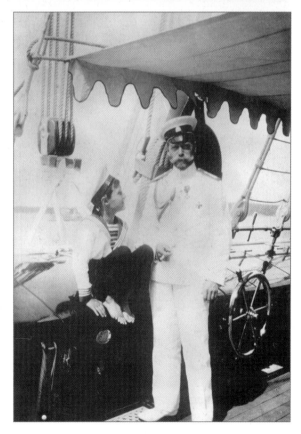

Often in summer the family would use the yacht to cruise the Finnish skerries, disembarking for fishing, picnics and games on land and sometimes for longer visits – a tradition dating back to the 1860s. In the photo on the left, the Tsaritsa is carried in a sling by two of the yacht's officers. In later years she was often carried over short distances or used a wheelchair because she was too ill to walk, but this was just for fun. The same page of her friend Anna Vyrubova's album shows other members of the party riding on the sling.

(*Above right*) Alexei at a family picnic, looking faintly disgruntled, and (*left*) posing on the shore with one of the ship's boys, who were his playmates.

The imperial couple were not the only ones to own a yacht. A pencilled caption on the back of this 1914 photograph of Grand Prince Nikolai Nikolaevich the younger and his wife Anastasia Nikolaevna reads, 'with his yacht at Valam 3 weeks before the War'.

Owning property overseas was more controversial. The imperial family had always travelled on a lavish scale in Europe, staying in hotels, rented villas or with relatives. But in 1897 Grand Prince Alexei Alexandrovich broke the pattern by buying a house in Paris. 'If it's true, one cannot but be amazed by such expenditure on the part of a Russian Grand Duke,' his cousin Konstantin Konstantinovich wrote – which may seem an unlikely remark, in view of the fabled wealth of the imperial family, but Konstantin and his brother Dmitri held firmly to the old view that the incomes of the family were meant to be used for the good of the country.

Grand Princess Vladimir owned a villa at Contrexéville on the Riviera, where this photograph was taken.

Another favourite place for late spring and early summer was the Alexandria Park at Peterhof. This belonged to the Dowager Tsaritsa but Nicholas and Alexandra had their own house built on the coast, the Alexandria Dacha or New Palace, where their three youngest children were born. (*Right*) Tatiana and Olga sit on one of the terraces with their cousin Princess Irina Alexandrovna (*centre*), and (*above*), Alexei, Anastasia and Maria play on the rocks below the house, on the shore of the Gulf of Finland.

The Crimean coast was the imperial family's autumn paradise for generations, and by the turn of the twentieth century many of the Grand Princes had their own residences there. This photograph of the Tsaritsa and her elder daughters was taken in 1909 on the terrace of Massandra, a French-style château built to the north-east of the resort town of Yalta for Alexander III. He intended it for his eldest son, but his early death meant that no one ever lived in the house. There was a working vineyard and the rose garden became famous, otherwise Massandra was simply a pleasant afternoon's outing from the palace of Livadia, on the other side of the town.

One of the main attractions of Livadia was the strip of private beach belonging to the estate. Here, in 1900, the little Grand Princesses Tatiana (*left*) and Olga play with buckets and toy watering cans watched by their nurse, while baby Maria is held in the arms of the nursery maid.

The Mikhailovichi had owned a Crimean estate since the 1860s. Ai Todor, to the south of Livadia along the coast, was inherited by Grand Prince Alexander Mikhailovich after his mother's death. He loved it: 'There was something hopeful and encouraging in being able to get up at sunrise and to say to myself, while riding along the bridle-path lined by jungles of wild roses: "This is real. This is mine. This will never turn on me. This is the place where I belong and where I should stay for ever."' The photograph, taken by a Yalta photographer, shows his elder children Andrei and Irina riding in the Crimean mountains in 1898.

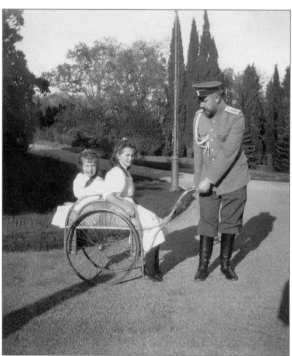

Three photographs taken at the old Livadia Palace in the autumn of 1909: (*above*) Anastasia and Alexei playing on the terrace; (*left*) Anastasia and Maria on a handcart drawn by Captain Drenteln; and (*below*) Alexei sailing his boat on the pond assisted by the sailor Derevenko (*right*) and watched by Count Frederiks and two other officers of the suite. The old palace at Livadia was built in the 1860s. The 1909 visit was the first the family had been able to make for some years and they found the building rather damp and neglected. As they left the demolition began and the new palace was completed in 1911.

Grand Duke Ernst Ludwig (*left*) and the Tsar running from the waves in 1912.

The Tsaritsa on the beach at Novy Svet on 24 May 1912.

Maria and Anastasia on the beach at Ayu Dag.

The new Livadia Palace in 1912: Alexei watches as Grand Prince Dmitri Pavlovich climbs back over the balustrade. Other photographs on the same page of Grand Duke Ernst Ludwig's album showed Dmitri walking on the roof – a stunt his little cousin probably envied. At this time Dmitri was very close to the imperial couple and many people believed that he would marry Grand Princess Olga.

Nicholas II and Princess Nina Georgievna in the garden of Harax, her father's Crimean house. In the last few years before the First World War the Tsar and Tsaritsa were close to Grand Prince Georgi Mikhailovich and his wife. They met for the last time in the Crimea in the summer of 1914 before the Tsar and his family left on *Shtandart*. Grand Princess Georgi's lady-in-waiting described the scene as the yacht sailed past Harax: 'He stood on the top deck, surrounded by the Empress, the four little Grand Duchesses in white and the Tzarevitch. . . . We waved and waved and could see through our glasses the Imperial family waving back. The last person I saw, although a dim, far-away figure, was His Majesty; the rest had gone below, but he remained and I saw him salute and then my eyes filled with tears.'

The Passing of Tsars

No crown, no amount of power or wealth can insulate the bearer from the ordinary tragedies of human life, and the imperial family knew its share of illness, accident and sorrow. But royal tragedy is never purely personal. However sharp the grief, it has to be played out with the nation looking on and, in some senses, sharing the loss. Since the time of Peter the Great, members of the imperial family were buried in the Fortress Cathedral of St Peter and St Paul in a timeless public ritual. Their tombs were ornamented with icons, with preserved wreaths and, over time, with wreaths of precious metals and gemstones: growing plants and cut flowers softened the cold marble. After the funeral of Alexander II it was found that visitors wanted to take away mementoes from his tomb and Princess Yurievskaya ordered that fresh flowers should be brought in every day. This was done for two months, until she refused to pay the bill. But still the visitors came and, in desperation, the commandant of the Fortress appealed for daily bouquets from the palace greenhouses. So the tombs had meaning for ordinary people: at the same time, the Cathedral was a place very personal to the family, for the living to return to, especially in times of stress or doubt.

Alexandra Feodorovna and her son on the balcony of the Alexander Palace in about 1909. Mention illness in the same breath as the Romanov dynasty and the word that springs most readily to mind is haemophilia. The last Tsesarevich, Nicholas II's only son Alexei, was haemophilic: it dominated his short life and had terrible consequences for his family. Haemophilia is a hereditary condition, a chemical imbalance in the blood which inhibits normal clotting. Any injury, particularly internal injury, can be dangerous; the sufferer also experiences frequent and unexplained bleeding into the joints, causing excruciating pain and temporary – possibly permanent – disability. Illness and infection can also bring on bleeding attacks. This was what Alexei lived with. His mother had to live with the knowledge that she had passed the condition to her son.

Alexei on the terrace of the new Livadia Palace in 1911. In other ways he was a tough little character: strong-willed – wilful, sometimes – and determined to rise above his condition and gain some semblance of normality. He responded eagerly to other people, lacking both the diffidence of his father and the crippling shyness of his mother, and his own experience of pain gave him compassion beyond his years. Courtiers detected a likeness to his great-grandfather Alexander II. Haemophilia was unknown in the Romanov family before Alexei. His mother had inherited the gene from her mother, and she from hers; it seems most likely that it had existed for centuries in Queen Victoria's female line ancestry. The final irony was that if Alexei had lived long enough to father a son – like his great-uncle Prince Leopold, Duke of Albany, who was also haemophilic – the child would have been perfectly healthy.

174

Alexandra with Alexei on the visit to Friedburg in 1910. The Tsaritsa's devotion to her son is well known. Having no practical remedy to turn to at times when his life was threatened she agonised over him, snatching at every thread of hope and losing much of her own strength and vitality in the process. She aged rapidly. Looking at some of the later photographs of Alexandra Feodorovna it is hard to remember that she never even reached the age of fifty.

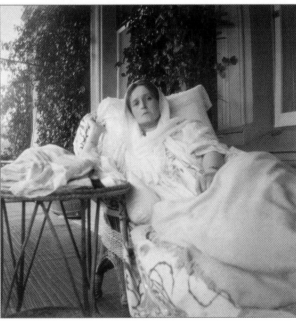

(*Above*) Alexandra on the balcony at Peterhof, alone and with Anastasia and Maria in about 1910/11. A question-mark still hangs over the Tsaritsa's own health. Many take it for granted that the problems she suffered – breathlessness, pains around the heart, general weakness – which made it increasingly difficult for her to perform her duties, were hysterical symptoms: the product of an unreasonable, some would say unbalanced mind. The fact remains that this is a pejorative judgement on Alexandra's character, not a medical assessment of her symptoms. It may be that she had a real physical condition. First, as a carrier of haemophilia, she would certainly have had a lower blood clotting factor than normal and could have experienced minor symptoms. Even as a very young woman, before her marriage, she suffered pains in her back and legs bad enough to require medical treatment.

Then there were the attacks of breathlessness, usually referred to in the language of the day as 'heart attacks'. Prince Roman Petrovich recounted an incident which happened at Djulber, his parents' Crimean home, on a summer evening when the Tsar and Tsaritsa had been invited to dinner. He was called in to greet them and all appeared well. Alexandra kissed him and spoke about her daughters, but he was still in the room when she was suddenly taken ill: 'She could not endure the summer heat, her face became red and she was unable to breathe. As soon as the doors and windows were thrown open, creating a through current of air, she started to recover.'

A curiously evocative image of the Tsar pushing his wife's wheelchair along one of the paths in the Alexander Park.

Alexandra had a good deal in common with her great-aunt, the Tsaritsa Maria Alexandrovna, seen here with her daughter Maria and son Pavel in 1877. Both were serious, reserved women who did not relate easily to Court and society, at their best when responding to someone else's need. But Maria had a readily identifiable illness, tuberculosis, which affected her from the age of twelve and had killed her mother in the previous year. The northern climate, grief for the premature deaths of two of her children, the pain of her husband's unfaithfulness (though she constantly forgave him), all these things sapped her strength and drove her ever more deeply into herself and her faith. The Tsar treated her with tenderness, tinged with guilt. In February 1880, when she lay close to death, a terrorist bomb damaged the private wing of the Winter Palace, narrowly missing the family. Alexander waited outside her room until she woke, so that she could see he was safe. At her request he took his mistress's children to meet her and she kissed and blessed them, crying as he too cried. But she died alone in her room in March 1880. Her children never forgot her. They had a cathedral built in Jerusalem in her memory and four years after her death her eldest surviving son would write, 'Whatever there is of love, goodness or honour in me I owe exclusively and alone to our dearly loved Mama. None of the teachers had influence over me, I loved none of them . . . they were no more than puppets to me – Mama constantly took trouble over us . . . she taught us to believe through her example and her deep Christian faith.'

The first severe blow to Maria Alexandrovna's strength and well-being was the death of her eldest child Alexandra, 'Lina', from tubercular meningitis at the age of six; decades later she could not speak of it without tears, but she was not the only mother in the imperial family to suffer such a loss. Her daughter-in-law Maria Feodorovna, seen here with her eldest son Nicholas in Denmark, gave birth in the year this photograph was taken to a second son, Alexander. He was bigger and more robust than his elder brother but succumbed to meningitis before his first birthday: 'The doctors maintain he did not suffer,' she told her mother, 'but we suffered terribly to see and hear him. . . . We have had him both drawn and photographed today so as at least to have some memory of him.'

Grand Princess Elizaveta Mavrikievna had nine children. Eight survived, but the eighth to be born, a girl christened Natalia, lived only two months – long enough to acquire a name and pet name, and that was all. In a family with so many boys, little girls were especially cherished. Her eleven-year-old brother Prince Oleg had been sent to the Crimea to escape the northern winter and noted sadly in his diary: 'So we never saw Natusya at all. She died on 10th May. She had peritonitis and inflammation of the brain . . . and she died in Mama's arms. Mama was the first to know that our dear little sister had passed away. She was born on the 10th of March, she was christened on the 10th of April and she died on the 10th of May: always the 10th.' He wrote to his father to ask for photographs of her.

Grand Princess Alexandra Georgievna, first wife of Grand Prince Pavel, was the only young mother to be lost to the family in childbirth in later years. In the autumn of 1891 she and her husband were staying with his brother Sergei and Elizaveta Feodorovna at Ilinskoe, as they often did. Alexei Volkov, Pavel's valet, described how Alexandra 'collapsed one day in the middle of a ball, in the grip of violent labour pains. . . . This sad accident was brought on by something unwise she had done the day before. At Ilinskoe there was a boat permanently moored on the bank of the Moskva and the Grand Princess often walked there with her friends. She never took the little path that led to the boat, but always jumped directly into it from a small projection of the bridge. This very day she did it again, despite the advanced stage of her pregnancy: the accident I have described and the premature birth of the child . . . was the result. Everything possible was attempted to save the Grand Princess. The efforts of doctors, the best that science could do, proved in vain: Grand Princess Alexandra Georgievna died after two days of terrible suffering.'

The tragedy left an indelible mark on all those closest to Alexandra. Pavel, seen here some months later with his children Maria and Dmitri, was inconsolable. His brother Sergei had to restrain him when her body was lowered into the tomb, and Volkov watched his health and spirits sink as the weeks passed: 'The doctors who cared for him . . . decided that the Grand Prince must go abroad to improve his physical health and restore the balance of mind and spirit. But an unexpected obstacle arose. The doctors ordered a course of massage during the journey and the Grand Prince absolutely refused to be treated by a newcomer, a stranger. It was Dr Turgenev who found a solution: he offered to spend a few days teaching me the art of medical massage. Our studies passed quickly and successfully, and to my duties as keeper of the Grand Prince's wardrobe were added those of masseur.

'Before going abroad, Grand Prince Pavel left his little children in the care of his brother Grand Prince Sergei Alexandrovich and the Grand Princess. In time the couple became very attached to their nephew and niece . . .'

But no tragedy would be further reaching in its effects than the loss of the Tsesarevich Nikolai in the spring of 1865. After celebrating his engagement to Princess Dagmar with his family in Darmstadt in October 1864, the Tsesarevich went on to Italy to continue the educational tour he had started some months before. In Florence he suddenly fell victim to back pain so severe that he had to be carried. He spent six weeks in bed, undergoing a series of painful treatments for a spinal abscess, and as soon as he could be moved he was taken to Nice, where his mother was spending the winter. There, French doctors disagreed with the diagnosis, viewing the 21-year-old's back pain as rheumatism and prescribing spinal massage. It was a mistake that cost Nikolai his life. Over the weeks the massage spread the infection into the surrounding tissue, then to the bone marrow and then to the brain. Nikolai's condition deteriorated steadily. His family gathered round him and medical specialists flocked to Nice but it was too late. Nikolai died on Sunday 24 April: the illustration below is an early documentary photograph of the funeral cortège in Nice. The body was taken home to Russia by sea, while the family travelled overland. 'This was a young man who personified all the hopes which a million brave men place in the future,' his tutor wrote. 'This was the symbol of all that is dear and sacred to us on this earth.'

Tuberculosis claimed the life of another Tsesarevich in the summer of 1899. Grand Prince Georgi Alexandrovich became Heir on his brother's accession but he had already lived away from St Petersburg for some years. His symptoms first became apparent in 1890; after that, he would never be fully well again. In 1891 he was moved to Abastuman in the Caucasus for the mountain air (*below*). Georgi lived an active life, mixing with local society and regiments; his sense of humour was irrepressible. He studied astronomy and built up a library on the history of the Caucasus. He enjoyed regular visits from the family, but his condition deteriorated all the time. In the summer of 1899, too weak to walk any distance, he took to riding a motor-bike. On 28 June/9 July 1899 he began to haemorrhage while riding and was found at the roadside by a peasant woman. He died soon after. It was one of history's ironies that Georgi, a perceptive, forceful character, felt by many to have been the son of Alexander III most fitted for the role of Tsar, should have been sidelined by illness. His was the brotherly support Nicholas II needed but never had.

The nineteenth century saw the loss of two teenage grandsons of Nicholas I through illness. Grand Prince Viacheslav Konstantinovich, 'Slava', the youngest child of the Admiral-General and something of a family pet, was taken ill very suddenly in February 1879, with a severe headache and sickness. He was sixteen. The day before, his mother is said to have seen a ghost in one of the galleries of Pavlovsk; a white lady, whose appearance was a foreshadowing of death. Viacheslav had an inflammation of the brain and he died within the week: 'Slava lay motionless with a large icon on the pillow,' his brother Konstantin wrote, 'and we did our best to help his breathing. They sent for Papa, Mama. . . . And then Dr Byttin said "This is the end". Papa didn't believe that it could be over so soon.' Then, walking in the funeral procession with his brother Dmitri and their father, Grand Prince Konstantin Nikolaevich, Konstantin was struck by a sad coincidence: 'Slava so loved to draw funeral processions with every detail of the ceremonial. . .'

Grand Prince Alexei Mikhailovich (*right*) was also a youngest child, of Grand Prince Mikhail Nikolaevich. 'A brilliant boy of liberal heart and absolute sincerity', according to his elder brother Alexander, Alexei had almost completed his naval officer's training at the time of his death. His cousin Kirill, a close contemporary on the training ships, remembered a brief holiday they had spent with Alexander III's family cruising off the Finnish skerries in the yacht *Tsarevna* in the summer of 1874; the Tsar organised a boat race for the two boys and his own son Mikhail which Kirill won. A few weeks later Alexei came down with what appeared to be a chill but was really tuberculosis. His health had never been good. Kirill would later say that Alexei's father refused to let him recuperate, insisting that it was his duty to finish his training. This may have been true in the initial stages but at some point the severity of Alexei's condition was realised; he was sent to San Remo, where he died on 2 March 1895. He was nineteen. 'The first time he wore his midshipman's uniform', Kirill wrote, 'was in his coffin.'

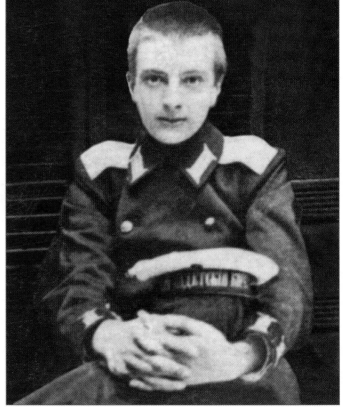

The death of Tsar Alexander III was also untimely, in its way, coming in the autumn of 1894 when the Tsar, a big man of prodigious strength, was only in his late forties. It was kidney disease that took him, in the small Heir's Palace at Livadia, which he preferred to the main palace even after his accession. The picture is a detailed engraving from a death-bed photograph: it was in this form that most people would have seen the early news photographs, published in illustrated journals.

Alexander's widow, Maria Feodorovna, arriving in her native Denmark soon after her husband's death. Her mother Queen Louise leads the group, walking beside her; among those following are her father King Christian IX, his brother Prince Hans of Schleswig-Holstein and his grandson Prince Christian of Denmark, Grand Prince Mikhail Alexandrovich and Prince Valdemar of Denmark. All are wearing the deep mourning black that custom demanded after a death; many widows wore it for the rest of their lives.

Alexei Mikhailovich's mother, Grand Princess Olga Feodorovna, had died some four years before him, the shortest-lived of Nicholas I's daughters-in-law. She complained of ill-health for years and chased an elusive cure around the spa towns of Europe. It was always said that a telegram bearing the news of her son Mikhail's illegal marriage prompted the heart attack that killed her, on a railway station in Kharkov, but, like so many similar stories, this is a distorted version of what happened. News of Mikhail's actions had already reached his parents in St Petersburg before his mother left for the Crimea. It was on this account that she left early and alone, on 28 March/9 April 1891, telling Maria Feodorovna that she was not feeling well and wanted time to recuperate in peace. She was taken ill on the train that same evening and returned to Kharkov some seven hours after first passing through the station. Doctors were called to her compartment and ordered her removal to the Tsar's waiting room. She remained there two full days, alone save for the servants, before her death on 31 March/12 April.

In contrast, her sister-in-law Grand Princess Alexandra Iosifovna was the longest-lived of their generation. She suffered a stroke towards the end of her life which left her unable to walk and so she remained at home, confined to a wheelchair and carefully protected by her family from sad or disturbing news. She died in her room in the Marble Palace in July 1911, two days before her eighty-first birthday.

Grand Princess Alexandra Iosifovna had outlived her husband by almost twenty years. Grand Prince Konstantin Nikolaevich (*right*) was a proud man, firmly adhering to the old values of duty and responsibility that he and his brothers had been taught in childhood. The death of Alexander II came as a body blow; still worse was the accession of the nephew he had never liked. He knew Alexander III wanted to be rid of him but refused to resign; 'My father bequeathed it to me to serve my deceased brother and his successors. Then my deceased brother entrusted me with the highest position in the Empire – that of the chairman of the State Council. In this position, and as Admiral-General, I am going to serve the new Emperor as well with all my zeal and devotion. In doing so I will fulfil my father's last wish . . .' Finally the decision was forced upon him; effectively dismissed after a lifetime of service, Konstantin retired to the Crimea with his mistress and their children. He returned home a few years before the end, following a stroke, to his wife and to a death-bed reconciliation with the Tsar, and died at Pavlovsk on 13/25 January 1892.

His son Konstantin Konstantinovich (*left*) also died at Pavlovsk in the summer of 1915, his health finally broken by the tragedies of the First World War. On the evening of 2/15 June he was resting in his study after a recent angina attack and his nine-year-old daughter Princess Vera was with him, reading, 'sitting on a little settee by the piano in front of the screen,' she told her brother, 'you know, in Papa's big cosy study in Pavlovsk. . . . Suddenly, I heard Papa gasping for breath. After hearing three or four more of those horrible gasps I rushed to Mama, to the bed-room where she was trying on a new coloured dress, probably for Ostashevo, where we were about to go because Papa was much better. . . . In such moments of fear a person is given extra powers. Mama could never understand how I had managed to open a heavy door with a mirror and green plants in front of it, the door between Papa's and Mama's studies. I ran up to Mama and cried, panting, "Papa hat keine Luft" [Papa cannot breathe]. Mama rushed after me but everything was over.' It must have been a terrifying experience for a child.

The funeral of Grand Prince Konstantin Konstantinovich in June 1915 was the last state funeral of imperial Russia. At first the coffin rested in the Italian Hall at Pavlovsk, guarded by representatives of regiments the dead man had served in and the military schools in his charge. On the eighth day it was taken by train to the capital and carried in solemn procession, with the men of the family following on foot. Prince Gavril's hand-written caption to this photograph identifies the place as the Fontanka Quay and the mourners as the Tsar himself, followed by Grand Princes Kirill Vladimirovich, Georgi Mikhailovich and Boris Vladimirovich in the first rank, from left to right, then by himself, his uncle Grand Prince Dmitri Konstantinovich and brothers Ioann and Konstantin in the second, then by Grand Prince Nikolai Mikhailovich. The funeral service took place the next day. At the last moment the family added a tribute of their own, personal to the dead man and very typical of him. Wherever he went the Grand Prince had treasured a small metal box of earth from Strelna, his birthplace. The box must have been a gift from his wife Elizaveta Mavrikievna; at least, on the lid was engraved in her handwriting a quotation from Lermontov: 'Can one ever forget one's Motherland, even for a moment?' The precious Strelna earth was scattered on the coffin lid.

Until the Revolution almost all the family lived out a peaceful existence, before the onset of illness or old age. But political violence was an increasing threat and its first target was, ironically, the country's greatest benefactor. Alexander II survived a long series of assassination attempts. He was asthmatic and the strain told on his health; he knew that sooner or later a terrorist would succeed. In a dangerous world his great comfort lay with Princess Yurievskaya and their children. This photograph, one of the last ever taken, shows the Tsar with the youngest, Ekaterina. On Sunday 1/13 March 1881 he signed a manifesto designed to set the country on the road to constitutional government; if he had lived, it would have been published the next day. Then he left the Winter Palace for a military parade: his nephew Dmitri Konstantinovich was to be duty officer for the first time. Next he visited his cousin Ekaterina Mikhailovna, and was returning home when a terrorist struck. Two bombs were thrown, the second of which caught the Tsar full in the lower part of the body; his brother Mikhail was among the first to reach the scene and rushed him back to the Winter Palace, but nothing could be done. The death-bed photograph (*below*) conceals the awful reality of the Tsar's injuries.

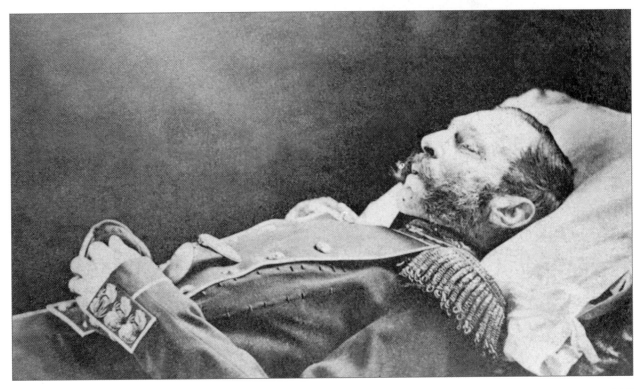

At the end of 1904 Grand Prince Sergei Alexandrovich resigned the Governor-Generalship of Moscow after thirteen years. Russia had suffered disastrously in the war against Japan and the country was in turmoil. Nicholas II felt obliged to make concessions but Sergei could not support them. He moved his family into the Kremlin for safety but continued to cross the city himself, to tidy up his affairs. Knowing the danger, he refused even to take an adjutant. On 4/17 February 1905, as his carriage approached the Nikolsky Gate of the Kremlin, a bomb was thrown, killing him outright. Two miles across the city the Kleinmichel children, who were friends of his wards, Maria and Dmitri, heard the explosion: 'I felt my heart sink and my hands and feet grow cold,' Olga Kleinmichel wrote after learning what had happened, 'realizing that the detonation we had just heard had meant the death of somebody – somebody we knew and loved.' Many Muscovites felt the same. Sergei's coffin lay in state in the Kremlin under a sea of funeral wreaths and 'every day the people were allowed in to pay their respects at specific hours; a hundred people were let in at a time. Services were held from morning to night, without interruption.'

Grand Princess Elizaveta Feodorovna in mourning. On the evening of the assassination the young Kleinmichels were taken to the first of the services. Olga described the hush that fell over the congregation as Elizaveta entered, 'the ribbon of the Order of St Catherine making a red streak across her black dress. I was afraid to look at her face; but, in spite of myself, I glanced up. She was very pale, but composed. Our young friends . . . Marie and her brother, Dmitri, followed. They looked as if they had been crying a great deal, but now their faces were only very serious. The nervous tension I was in broke down when the service began and I cried as I had never done before.' Olga paid tribute to the manner in which Elizaveta bore the shock and pain of loss. The rest of the Grand Princess's life became a sustained tribute to Sergei Alexandrovich and the years they had spent together. From the moment she helped to gather the remains of his body from the snow she showed a courage and a depth of love few could have matched – or even understood.

Elizaveta with Marie and Dmitri. Three days after her husband's death the Grand Princess visited the assassin in prison because she knew it was what Sergei would have wanted, to give the man a chance of forgiveness. 'I am quite calm and happy,' she told her brother, 'yes, happy to know that my darling is at peace near God, and that he is spared this awful time.' She was granted guardianship of Maria and Dmitri, in partnership with the Tsar. 'May God guide and help us to bring up Marie and Dmitri as well as Sergei had begun,' she wrote. 'I will do my best and knowing his ideas and principles, only need try and follow what has always been before my eyes.' She withdrew progressively from society, devoting herself first to the care of the war-wounded at Ilinskoe, then to a longer term plan to care for the most deprived people of Moscow through a religious house of her own foundation: a convent of a type unknown in Russia where the motivation was not contemplative but practical. Several years of study were needed on her part before the idea could take concrete form.

Elizaveta and Dmitri in 1908, in the window corner of her sister's Mauve Boudoir. Young Maria Pavlovna had always resented her aunt and uncle, blaming them for her father's desertion because she could not bear to blame him. She believed that Dmitri shared her feelings but it may not have been the case: there is no direct evidence of Dmitri's feelings, but he seems to have been closer to his aunt, the only mother he had ever known. Photographs like this one, from Grand Duke Ernst Ludwig's album, bear out the impression. When Elizaveta finally withdrew into the Martha and Mary Convent in 1910, taking the veil with the first group of nuns, she passed to him the properties she had inherited from her husband.

Elizaveta Feodorovna as a nun – even the habits of her order were new to Russia, where nuns were typically covered in heavy black robes reaching to the floor, topped with a tall veiled hat. The nuns of the Martha and Mary Convent wore grey or white in simple flowing lines (the habit was, in fact, artist-designed especially for the Convent). When this novelty was questioned by the male authorities of the Holy Synod, Elizaveta told them that the new habits were more practical for the hospital. Her nuns were better fed and allowed to sleep through the night because they needed their strength for a hard working day. She was right, but the plan might never have been approved if the Tsar had not stepped in to establish the foundation by decree.

Elizaveta's sister-in-law, Grand Princess Maria Pavlovna the elder, with her granddaughter Kira. Grand Prince Vladimir died suddenly of a cerebral haemorrhage in February 1909 and Maria Pavlovna wore mourning for him for the rest of her life. Her style of mourning, however, was quite different from that of Elizaveta or even of her old rival, the Dowager Tsaritsa. She absolutely refused to withdraw. Dreading solitude, she filled her time with parties and receptions. Her charity bazaars, held annually in the House of the Nobility, were key events in the social calendar; she took over her husband's role as President of the Academy of Arts and saw herself in many ways as a social leader, going her own way with absolute confidence. She was neither kind nor forgiving, but she had style. If many people saw her as a rival to the two Tsaritsas it was because she clearly came to see herself in that light. She did her utmost too to push her sons to the fore, but they never lived up to her ambitions.

War and Revolution

The military uniforms worn by Romanov princes from boyhood were not just symbolic. Each generation save the last and youngest gave active service to Russia on a long succession of battlefields – in wars against Turkey, war in the Caucasus and the Crimea, war against Japan: maintaining a powerful empire was a costly business. Then, as nationalism became a force in Europe and tensions grew between nations, the imperial family was drawn into that other war that beset nineteenth-century royalty, when cousin fought against cousin and brother against brother-in-law, and loyalties unquestioned for years were shaken to their foundations. Years of intermarriage had enmeshed the family firmly into the international family of royalty, whose members conversed freely in several languages. In peacetime it had never mattered: it even seemed to guarantee that peace would endure. But it made war especially traumatic and dangerous for all members of that international family, women as well as men. For them too, war imposed heavier demands to support medical services, to raise funds, and to do whatever lay within their power to lift morale. War strains the resources of any country. In the early years of the twentieth century the strain was too much for Russia and twice, in 1905 and 1917, war led directly into revolution. The second time proved fatal.

Alexander II and his staff in headquarters at Gorny Studen in Bulgaria during the Russo–Turkish War of 1877–8. (*From the left*) the Tsar's nephew Prince Alexander of Battenberg (*in front*); Prince Suvorov; Prince Carol of Romania; the Tsar and Grand Prince Nikolai Nikolaevich the elder (*see left also*). For centuries the Turks had ruled in the Balkans and Russia fought a series of wars against them, motivated by her own ambitions in the area and by concern for the suffering of Orthodox Christians. Brutal suppression by the Turks of a riot in Herzogovina was the spark which lit the 1877 war; Alexander II was reluctant to fight but public outrage in Russia and the inability of the European powers to agree concerted action forced his hand. After terrible reverses his armies won through, under the command of his brother Grand Prince Nikolai, aided by Prince Carol's Romanians. But when it seemed that Russia might do too well out of the war, with Alexander of Battenberg established as prince of a newly independent Bulgaria and Constantinople itself open to Russian troops, a British naval force was sent into the Black Sea, including the Tsar's son-in-law Prince Alfred and his nephew Prince Louis of Battenberg.

Another nephew of the Tsar, Duke Sergei of Leuchtenberg (*right*), fought in the Russian XII Corps in Bulgaria under the command of his cousin, the Tsesarevich Alexander. On 24 October XII Corps was ordered to take advantage of a Turkish withdrawal and advance towards Basarbowa and Iovan-Tschiflik. Fighting near Basarbowa became intense; Sergei was leading a reconnaissance when a Turkish bullet caught him in the head. He was twenty-six years old and had spent long periods in Italy; unlike other members of the family, the Tsesarevich included, who had been fiercely pro-war, fighting to him had been a duty only. A friend remembered him as 'a thorough West European, an artist, elegant and clever. All his sympathies were with Italy, the home of art, science and culture, "but for these Bulgarians, Serbs and other Slavs," he said to me, "I have not the slightest sympathy."'

Grand Prince Sergei Alexandrovich, his cousin, was another of the young men of the family who saw battle for the first time in the Russo–Turkish War. He shared Sergei Leuchtenberg's love of Italy and its culture, but what he felt about fighting in the Balkans we don't know, as so few of his personal documents have been put on record. But he was close to his mother and she was ardently in favour of the war, urged on by the family's confessor, Father Bazhanov, who saw the freeing of Balkan Christians as a religious duty. Sergei Alexandrovich left for the front with his father in the spring of 1877. In later years he wore the medal of the Order of St George, always awarded for bravery on the battlefield.

Grand Prince Alexei Alexandrovich, Admiral General of the Russian navy (*left, in the white cap*), Nicholas II (*centre*) and Count Frederiks leaving the Alexander Nevsky Cathedral in Reval on 27 September/10 October 1904. At this time Russia was again at war, now with Japan. The roots of the conflict lay in Russia's ambitions in the Far East, which the Japanese contested: it began with a surprise Japanese attack on the Russian naval base at Port Arthur.

Grand Prince Alexei found himself presiding over a series of naval disasters which were not of his making but for which he would bear ultimate responsibility. He sent his nephew, Grand Prince Kirill (*left*), to serve under Admiral Makarov, a first-rate officer he placed in command of Port Arthur after the first attack. Kirill served on Makarov's flagship *Petropavlovsk*. But on 13/26 April 1904 the ship struck a mine, detonating all the munitions on board. Kirill's brother Boris was watching from land and saw the horror: 'Where the *Petropavlovsk* had been but a few seconds before there was now nothing but a sinister pall of black smoke. Then there was another fearful explosion; and about a minute later . . . we saw that the *Petropavlovsk* was disappearing into the sea bows first, with her propellers turning in the air as her stern pointed skyward. It was a fearful impression.' Kirill jumped clear just in time, but over six hundred men were lost, including Admiral Makarov and his senior staff. With them went any hope of a Russian victory. The humiliation felt in Russia over the relentless catalogue of defeats precipitated the 1905 Revolution.

On the outbreak of war in 1914 Grand Prince
Nikolai Nikolaevich the younger was called on
by the Tsar to take up the position his father
had occupied in 1877, in command of Russia's
armies. 'Words could not express what I felt in
that moment,' he said. 'The appointment, and
all it entailed, struck as a bolt of lightning
through my head, leaving an indescribable
exuberance, never to be forgotten. I replied that
for me the will of His Majesty was as a Divine
command, and so it would remain.' After
several hours with the Tsar he returned to his
wife, brother and sister-in-law and their
children, and prayed with them in his estate
chapel before leaving to set up his first
headquarters. His German orders and uniforms
– a legacy of the peace-time world of royalty –
were thrown away or burned.

Nicholas II reviewing troops on the Eastern Front. In the summer of 1914, with the German armies
moving rapidly across France and the Low Countries, the French called on Russia for help and Nikolai
ordered a massive invasion of East Prussia. His armies made initial progress before suffering a catastrophic
defeat – but the Allies in the west were given the time they needed to halt the German advance.

The Tsar (*right*) and Grand Prince Nikolai (*left, beside the horses*) on the Eastern Front.

The Commander-in-Chief in the field: Nikolai (*right, seated*) with some of his officers in Poland in 1915.

War had barely started when five sons of Grand Prince Konstantin Konstantinovich, Princes Ioann, Gavril, Konstantin, Oleg and Igor, left together for the front to serve with the Guards. In the heady atmosphere of the day this seemed inspiring and crowds gathered to cheer them off. A commemorative postcard was produced, but before it could be issued tragedy had overtaken the family. Prince Oleg, aspiring poet and writer, the Grand Prince's acknowledged favourite and the only Romanov prince to have received a civilian education, was wounded in an attack on a German position in East Prussia on 27 September/10 October. By the time anyone realised how serious the wound was, blood poisoning had set in; Oleg was moved to Vilna for an emergency operation but he could not be saved. The same confident patriotism remained with him to the end: 'I am so happy. . . . It will encourage the troops to know that the Imperial House is not afraid to shed its blood.' Oleg lived just long enough to see his parents and to receive from his father the medal of the Order of St George; by his own request he was buried on the banks of the River Ruza, in the Moscow countryside.

The photographs show Oleg in camp in February 1914 (*right*); on his death-bed (*below, right*) and on a memorial postcard sold to raise funds for his mother's war work.

The Tsaritsa Alexandra in the uniform of a Red Cross nurse. In wartime Alexandra came into her own. When confronted with another person's need, for which she could give practical help, she forgot the shyness which was usually such a handicap. She and her elder daughters trained as probationary nurses and worked in the military hospital in the Catherine Palace in Tsarskoe Selo. They took and passed the same examinations as any other probationer, wore the uniform and treated the wounded. 'To some it may seem unnecessary my doing this,' Alexandra wrote, 'but I can much better then look after my hospital here, and help is much needed, and every hand is useful.' She made regular visits to hospitals in St Petersburg and beyond. It was a genuine response to the war but, by its very nature, a private one. In society there were indeed people who thought it beneath the dignity of a Tsaritsa.

Grand Princesses Olga (*right*) and Tatiana Nikolaevna with some of their patients (one of whom is holding a camera).

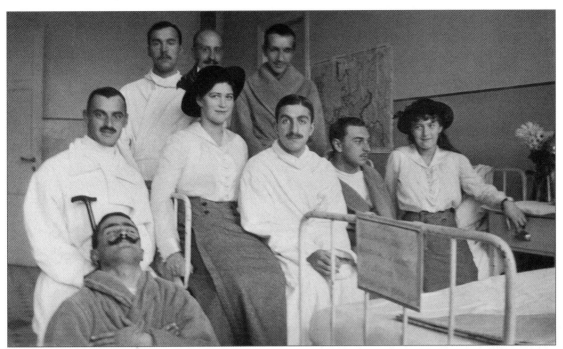

Maria and Anastasia Nikolaevna were too young to nurse, but a hospital was established under their patronage in the Feodorovsky Village in Tsarskoe Selo, close to the Alexander Palace, and they took great delight in visiting and performing small tasks for the wounded – reading, letter-writing, arranging flowers – just as another girl very much of their age, the future Queen Elizabeth the Queen Mother, was doing for the wounded in her father's house at Glamis. All over Europe women and girls served the war effort in this, the only way open to them.

Alexei with Joy, his spaniel, in a photograph taken by his mother in 1916 and published to benefit war charities. The family had become quite astute in their use of private photographs and films. In November 1915 Alexandra wrote to her husband, 'How charming Alexei's photos are, the one standing ought to be sold as a postcard – *both* might be really – please, be done with Baby, also for the public and then we can send them to the soldiers.' 'Baby' was the family's name for Alexei, who had gone to the front with his father. Some movie footage had been taken of him playing with his dog which Alexandra had not seen but thought of releasing. But she knew that Alexei was not impressed. He thought 'that the dog looked cleverer than he'!

Grand Princess Olga Alexandrovna followed her regiment, the 12th Akhtyrsky Hussars, at the start of the war. She took up nursing in a Red Cross hospital at Rovno, close to the border of Poland and Austria, refusing all the privileges of rank. She shared a room with another nurse and worked on the wards, once joining her brother for victory celebrations at Lemberg in Galicia. Then, in the late summer of 1915, after a series of overwhelming defeats, the army withdrew and the hospital was moved back to Kiev where conditions and morale worsened all the time. The old certainties no longer seemed to apply. In the spring of 1916 Olga petitioned her brother for a divorce from Prince Peter of Oldenburg and permission to marry Nikolai Kulikovsky, whom she had loved for some years. The Tsar agreed when he visited Kiev in September; it was the last time brother and sister would ever meet.

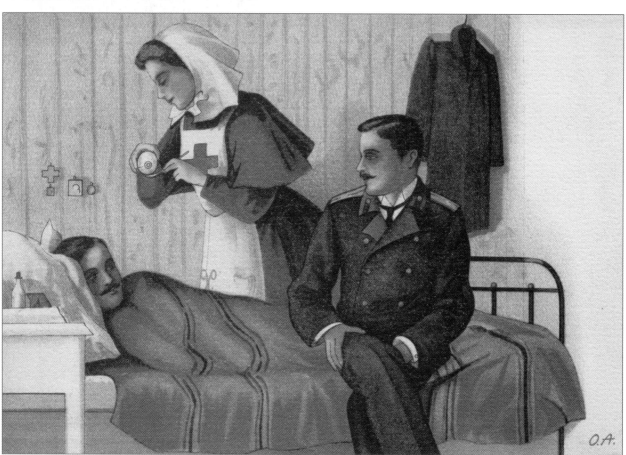

Olga proved to be a skilled nurse, with real sympathy for the men in her charge and no fear of the horrors she witnessed. But she did not forget her other skills and put her gift for watercolour painting to good use, producing a series of lively illustrations to be sold as postcards in aid of her charities. Most showed landscape or unrelated scenes; this one is interesting because it reflects her experience of nursing.

Maria Pavlovna the elder, Grand Princess Vladimir, embodied a concept and style of royalty totally alien to Olga or to the Tsaritsa. She threw herself into war work of a very different kind, as the glamorous and self-possessed figurehead of a network of ambulance trains and flying hospitals originally set up during the war against Japan. She made no secret of her contempt for Alexandra, though the war years did see a brief and hesitant rapprochement between them. But within her own sphere Maria Pavlovna was superb. A courier from the British Foreign Office, Albert Stopford, accompanied her with her ambulance train to Dvinsk and he watched her speak to the wounded and oversee their transfer to hospital; 'It was the most divine time being with her,' he wrote: 'She is a marvellous woman, and always at her best when there is much to do – sparing herself no trouble.'

Maria Georgievna, Grand Princess Georgi Mikhailovich, was in England when the war began, ostensibly taking her younger daughter for a cure in Harrogate, though she was also glad to have time away from her husband. Finding it impossible to return to Russia on the outbreak of war, she opened a military hospital in Harrogate, raising funds from among friends and family and also from local people. She undertook a preliminary Red Cross nursing course for which she was given a certificate, though she does not appear to have worn uniform. Her work expanded through the war years and in 1919 the local paper acknowledged the town's debt: 'In reviewing all that has been done to ameliorate the suffering of our sick and wounded, we must pay grateful thanks to the Grand Duchess George for undertaking a great and noble work.'

All the women of the family played some part in relief work, whether or not they chose to do hands-on nursing. Grand Princess Anastasia Nikolaevna, wife of Nikolai Nikolaevich, the Commander-in-Chief, is photographed here with the Minister of War, General Sukhomlinov (*on the extreme right*), at the handing over of a new Red Cross train bearing her name. She and her sister Militsa also supported the military hospitals around Kiev. But this photograph conceals an uncomfortable reality. Long before the war Sukhomlinov and the Grand Prince had been constantly at odds. As war progressed it was unhelpful, to say the least, to have Army Headquarters, in the person of Nikolai Nikolaevich, on bad terms with the War Ministry. After the military disasters of 1915 the Duma, who were close to the Grand Prince, accused the War Minister of spying.

It was around this time that the Tsar chose to take overall command of the army. He had always intended to do it. At heart, he believed that it was his place to be at the front with his men. The great retreat was over and he hoped that his coming might inspire a change of mood – but at the same time he could not help being aware that other members of the family, including his wife, did not trust Nikolai and accused him of building up an alternative power base. For the Grand Prince dismissal came as a bitter blow, though he accepted it without complaint. The photo shows him on his way to his new appointment as Viceroy of the Caucasus. Inexorably the imperial family was splitting into separate camps.

The whole Nikolaevich clan – the Grand Prince, his brother Grand Prince Peter, who had served on his staff from the outbreak of war, both their wives and Peter's family – all transferred to the Caucasus on Nikolai's appointment. Peter's son Prince Roman (*above, right*), served with Caucasian troops near Trabzon and his elder daughter Marina found nursing work with the same unit. Their sister Nadejda (*above, left*) was just too young to have undertaken nursing training; engaged to Prince Oleg Konstantinovich just before the outbreak of war, in April 1917 in the Crimea she married Prince Nikolai Orlov.

The Tsar's entire family, (*seated in the centre, from the left*) Tatiana, Anastasia, Maria, Olga, the Tsar, the Tsaritsa and Alexei, visiting the Tsaritsa's hospital in the Crimea in 1916.

Even the stress of war could not turn the more recalcitrant ducklings into swans. Grand Prince Boris Vladimirovich had been a playboy all his adult life and he saw no reason to change. He entered the war as commander of the Guards Regiment of Ataman Cossacks but managed to stay far from the fighting. His behaviour towards the Allies was so insulting that in July 1916 the British Ambassador made a formal protest. The French Ambassador remarked in his diary, 'Nothing will come of the remonstrances. Boris Vladimirovich will calmly continue his life of pleasure and idleness. What has he been doing since the war began? Nothing. . . . How comes it that this prince of thirty-seven, strong and healthy, loaded with wealth and privileges, has not claimed his share in the marvellous effort of endurance, heroism and self-sacrifice the Russian nation has made without flinching for nearly two years.'

Understandably, when Boris's mother Maria Pavlovna suggested a marriage between him and Grand Princess Olga, the Tsaritsa (*seen here with her husband*) was appalled: 'An inexperienced young girl would suffer terribly, to have her husband 4, or 5th hand or more.' With the Tsar at the front, more and more responsibility devolved on to Alexandra. It was more than she could handle and it left her open to blame for the country's problems, even from within the family.

The end is all too well known. The country was strained to breaking point by the war, and with rising unrest on the home front an exhausted regime simply ran out of answers. Some members of the imperial family pushed for last-minute constitutional change, as in 1905. Some formed their own conspiracy – but it was too late. In February 1917 senior army commanders urged the Tsar to abdicate and he gave way, nominating his brother Mikhail as his successor. He felt betrayed, and did not want to risk losing Alexei to his enemies. He was imprisoned with his family, first in the Alexander Palace – where the photograph on which this painting was based was taken, showing (*from the left*) Maria, Anastasia, Tatiana, the Tsar and several guards. In 1918 the family was moved east, first to Tobolsk, then to Ekaterinburg where, on the night of 4/17 July, they were murdered with their doctor and three faithful attendants.

Grand Prince Mikhail Alexandrovich had been allowed to return to Russia on the outbreak of war and had served with distinction as a front-line officer. After talking to leading figures from the Duma, the Russian parliament, he refused to take up the throne unless his accession was confirmed by the people. Seven months later the Bolshevik Revolution ensured that no one would ever ask them. In March 1918 Mikhail was exiled to Perm with his secretary; both were murdered in woodland outside the town in the early hours of 13/26 June.

The Tsar and his brother were not the only victims. In March 1918 all members of the imperial family were ordered to report to the secret police headquarters in the capital for registration. When they did so, the healthier and younger men were given only a few hours to prepare for deportation to Siberia. Grand Prince Sergei Mikhailovich (*left*) and his secretary, the brothers Ioann (*below left*), Konstantin (*below right, seated*) and Igor Konstantinovich (*below right*), and Prince Vladimir Paley (*facing page, above*) were in the party that left by train on the evening of 22 March/ 4 April, bound first for Viatka, then Ekaterinburg, where they were joined by Grand Princess Elizaveta Feodorovna (*facing page, above right*) and one of her nuns. In May the whole party was moved to Alapaevsk, where they were imprisoned in the schoolhouse for two months. They were murdered in a mineshaft in surrounding woodland on the night following the deaths of the imperial family.

Grand Prince Pavel Alexandrovich (*right*) was a
sick man in 1918, with symptoms variously
ascribed to tuberculosis or cancer. Too ill to
register with other members of the family, he
remained under observation at Tsarskoe Selo
with Princess Paley and their daughters. On
5/18 July 1918 – the very day of his son
Vladimir's murder, though he could not
know it – he witnessed the christening
of his grandchild Roman, the child of
his elder daughter Maria Pavlovna the
younger and Prince Putiatin. But he
must have sensed what was coming.
One of his younger daughters recalled a
walk in the garden: 'He spoke to us at
length about all that he owed to our
mother, all that she had brought to him
which he had never known in his life
before, and about all that she had been to
him. He spoke while he walked, and this
allowed him to overcome his reserve and his
intense shyness. Did he sense then that he had
not long to live? I am tempted to believe it
and to think that he was asking us to take care
of our mother when he could no longer be
with her.'

Grand Prince Pavel was arrested at the end of July 1918 and taken to the old secret police headquarters on Gorohovaia Street in the capital for three weeks, then moved to the Schpalernaia Prison where his cousins, Grand Princes Nikolai Mikhailovich (*left*), Georgi Mikhailovich (*below left*) and Dmitri Konstantinovich (*below*) were already being held. For some time the four cousins occupied the same corridor before Pavel was moved back to Gorohovaia Street on 15/28 January 1919; the others were transferred to the Troubetskoy Bastion in the Peter and Paul Fortress. Pavel joined them the next day. In the early hours of 17/30 January the four men were shot beside an open grave in the square in front of the Peter and Paul Cathedral, which for generations had been the honoured burial place of their family.

12

Full Circle

Two distinct groups of the family found their way to the Crimean coast before the Bolshevik Revolution. The Dowager Tsaritsa, her daughters and their families settled at Ai Todor, while the Nikolaevich clan took up residence in their own houses a few miles to the west. Soon both groups were placed under house arrest. For years, contact between the Nikolaevichi and the rest of the family had been only minimal, but a new understanding developed under duress. In February 1918 all the prisoners were concentrated at Djulber, Grand Prince Peter's home. They were guarded by men of the Sevastopol Soviet, who would not shoot them without express orders, but the nearby Yalta Soviet were bent on killing. With Germans advancing towards the Crimea the Yalta men decided to act: for ten nights the younger prisoners helped to guard Djulber against an expected attack. But the murderers were delayed when their car hit a mountain wall and it was the Germans who arrived first: the prisoners were saved.

Others had to contrive their own escape. Some were helped by foreign diplomats, some by sympathetic locals: in all, forty-four members of the imperial family came out of Russia alive. But they faced an uncertain future, without homes, status or nationality, cast ashore in a world that no longer wanted to know them.

For some months the Crimea was safe and the prisoners were able to return to their separate houses. But the Germans were losing the war and without them danger would return. In November 1918 a British naval detachment arrived with offers of sanctuary from relatives in the west; Grand Prince Alexander Mikhailovich left with his eldest son but the others preferred to stay. The danger grew. Early in 1919 a second British offer of help came with the ship HMS *Marlborough*; this time Maria Feodorovna did not refuse, though she insisted that space must be found for all those who wished to leave. The photo above shows her with Grand Prince Nikolai Nikolaevich (*see also left*) on board *Marlborough* on 26 March/8 April. Prince Roman captured the scene three days later as the ship sailed: 'Into our field of vision came a great freight and passenger ship . . . the last ships with emigrants on board. The freight ship drew near us and slid slowly past: suddenly we could hear the notes of "God Save the Tsar" – it was the refugees who were singing. They had recognised the Dowager Tsaritsa and Uncle Nikolasha standing by the railing. My uncle . . . saluted, raising his hand to his astrakhan cap, and the Tsaritsa made the sign of the cross.'

Grand Princess Ksenia's sons by the rail of HMS *Marlborough*. (*In front, left to right*) Feodor, Dmitri, Nikita, Rostislav and Vasili. In the background is Yalta.

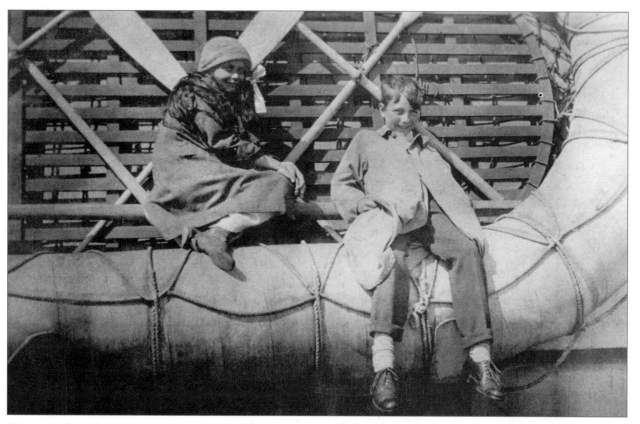

Prince Vasili with Princess Sofie Dolgoruky in one of the ship's lifeboats. Sofie's uncle, Prince Sergei Dolgoruky, was Master of the Household to the Dowager Tsaritsa and also escaped on *Marlborough* with his mother and daughter. In later years Sofie would write a book, *Sofka, the Autobiography of a Princess*.

Princess Nadejda Petrovna on board HMS *Marlborough* on 8 April, 'snapped in a position of ease', as the postcard's original caption read. Nadejda married Prince Nikolai Orlov in April 1917 and their baby daughter Irina was the ship's youngest passenger.

At Constantinople Grand Princes Nikolai and Peter, with their wives, Peter's elder children and others of their party, left *Marlborough* and transferred to HMS *Nelson*, leaving Nadejda with the Orlovs. The ship was to take them to Italy where the King and Queen – a younger sister of Grand Princesses Militsa and Anastasia – had offered refuge. This group was taken on HMS *Nelson* and shows (*in front, from the left*) Baroness Maria Stahl (a childhood friend of Peter's children; her father was his adjutant. Her mother, Grand Princess Militsa's lady-in-waiting, was a granddaughter of the poet Pushkin: both parents are likely to be in the photograph); unidentified lady; Grand Princess Anastasia and Grand Prince Nikolai; Grand Princess Militsa and Grand Prince Peter; Princess Marina. Prince Roman is behind on the extreme right.

Grand Princess Elizaveta Mavrikievna with her daughters Princess Tatiana (*on the sofa*) and Princess Vera (*in front*), her youngest son Prince Georgi and her grandchildren Teymuraz and Nathalie Bagration-Mukhransky (Princess Tatiana's children) in Brussels in 1921. In five years Elizaveta Mavrikievna lost her son and son-in-law in battle, her husband to the combined effects of heart disease and grief, three more sons to the murderers at Alapaevsk and her brother-in-law in the Fortress. With her younger children and grandchildren Vsevelod and Ekaterina, Prince Ioann's son and daughter, she had managed a precarious existence in the Marble Palace, 'stealing' her own possessions to sell for food. Part of the building was taken over by Bolsheviks and, with conditions worsening all the time, in October 1918 she accepted an offer of help from the Queen of Sweden. Swedish diplomats obtained permission for her to leave with Georgi and Vera, the grandchildren and four members of the household, and passage was arranged on the Swedish ship *Angermanland*.

The journey was dangerous. The passengers and their luggage were searched on boarding – even Princess Vera's spectacle frames were examined – but the Grand Princess had been canny enough to send any valuables with Swedish officials. She and her family could not escape the attention of a Soviet agent on board the ship and the *Angermanland* was halted twice – once by the Soviets and once by the Germans. The weather was against them too, and the voyage took eight days.

Princess Tatiana was helped out of Russia with Teymuraz, Nathalie and their governess by Alexander Korotchenzov, Grand Prince Dmitri Konstantinovich's faithful ADC. She was ill at the time, and frequently had to be moved on a stretcher. In November 1921, encouraged by the Grand Princess and Queen Olga of Greece, Tatiana married Korotchenzov in Geneva. He died just three months later. Years after, once her children had grown, Tatiana became a nun.

Her sister-in-law Princess Elena Petrovna, Vsevelod and Ekaterina's mother, had the most extraordinary escape of all. She had followed Prince Ioann to Siberia voluntarily and was allowed to leave the schoolhouse at Alapaevsk to return to her children. But local Bolsheviks arrested her at Ekaterinburg and put her in the ordinary prison at Perm; she remained there until the Norwegians traced her and had her moved. She was then held hostage in the Kremlin Palace before finally being allowed to leave; she joined the Grand Princess and her children in Sweden.

(*Above left*) Grand Prince Kirill and his son
Vladimir, who was born in exile in Finland in
August 1917. To some, the birth of a son to
the next Grand Prince in the male line
seemed to hold promise for the future and
photos of Vladimir like the one on the right,
with the imperial eagle on the little boy's
shield, were produced as postcards by the
Anti-Bolshevist Committee in Paris in the
1920s. In 1924 Kirill proclaimed himself
'Emperor and Autocrat of all the Russias' but
not all the survivors were willing to support
him. There were various reasons; most
immediate, perhaps, was the way in which he
and his wife Victoria Melita (*left*) had
welcomed the February Revolution. A letter
she sent to her sister at the time makes it clear
how deeply implicated they were. Their
house was surrounded by the mob, she said,
'yet heart and soul we are with this
movement of freedom which at the same
time probably signs our own death warrant. . . .
We personally are losing all, our lives are
changed at one blow and yet we are almost
leading the movement.'

Kirill's mother, Grand Princess Maria Pavlovna the elder, at Contrexéville. She had left the capital in February 1917 for the Caucasus and had endured an extraordinary catalogue of privations and dangers, despite her age. Her flawless self-confidence never deserted her. Encountering her by chance in the port of Novorossisk at the start of 1920, her niece Grand Princess Olga Alexandrovna was impressed, almost in spite of herself. 'I felt proud of her,' Olga would later recall. 'Disregarding peril and hardship, she stubbornly kept to all the trimmings of bygone splendour and glory. And somehow she carried it off. . . . For the first time in my life I found it was a pleasure to kiss her.' Maria Pavlovna left on an Italian liner in February, but her years as a fugitive had taken their toll. She fell ill a few months later and died at Contrexéville in September 1920.

With the Grand Princess during her adventures in the Caucasus were her sons Boris and Andrei and their mistresses – who had always to be housed in a separate building because Maria Pavlovna would not acknowledge their existence. Mathilde Kschessinskaya, still with Andrei, left an account of all that happened to them in her autobiography, *Dancing in Petersburg*. Having been loved as a young woman by the future Tsar Nicholas II, and protected for years by his cousin Grand Prince Sergei Mikhailovich, in exile she married Andrei. She taught ballet for many years and Margot Fonteyn was one of her pupils. The photo shows her in old age with her son Vladimir.

Grand Princess Olga Alexandrovna, Nikolai Kulikovsky and their sons Tihon (*right*) and Guri in about 1930. Because she was married to a commoner, Olga escaped imprisonment at Djulber with her mother and was allowed to live in relative safety with her husband and baby. Following the German surrender, the Kulikovskys left Yalta by steamer for Novorossisk and lived for a time in the Caucasus, where their second son was born. But it became too dangerous to stay and, with the help of some loyal Cossacks, the family made their way back to Novorossisk – a winter journey lasting two months. They sailed on a merchant ship in February 1920 and finally reached Denmark and the Dowager Tsaritsa on Good Friday that year. Denmark was to be their home until 1948, when the country was under German occupation. Once again they were forced to leave, this time for Canada, where Olga stayed for the rest of her life. Her memoirs, as recorded by Ian Vorres in *Once a Grand Duchess*, remain one of the most sympathetic accounts of the imperial family, and an exhibition of her paintings in Moscow in 2002 has shown just how gifted an artist she was.

Grand Prince Dmitri Pavlovich was sent by the Tsar to the Persian front in January 1917 for his part in the murder of Rasputin. Many relatives protested, but when the February Revolution broke it proved the saving of Dmitri. The Provisional Government would have welcomed him back but he was still loyal to the Tsar and would be haunted for the rest of his life by the murder. He escaped to Teheran, where the British Legation gave him sanctuary and emotional support. In November 1918 the British Minister Sir Charles Marling and his wife took Dmitri to London. Though he was seen by many in the diplomatic community as a potential claimant to the Russian throne, and by many mothers as a good catch, he remained insecure. He drifted. In 1926 he married Audrey Emery, an American heiress, and they had a son, Paul (*below*). But the marriage failed and shortly before the Second World War Dmitri saw his son off at the docks at Genoa, bound for a new life in America. Paul (*below right*) would one day become Mayor of Palm Beach. Dmitri died in a sanatorium in Davos in March 1942.

It is said that on 30 May/12 June 1918 Prince Andrei Alexandrovich, eldest son of Alexander Mikhailovich and Grand Princess Ksenia, married Elizaveta Fabrizievna di Sasso-Ruffo in the house chapel at Ai-Todor, with his brothers Feodor and Nikita and Prince Roman Petrovich as his supporters (see Notes, p. 237). The young couple certainly left the Crimea by sea with Grand Prince Alexander in November 1918 and their first child, Ksenia (*above, with her mother*), was born in Paris in March 1919.

Andrei and Elizaveta with Ksenia and their son Michael in about 1922. Elizaveta developed cancer in the late 1930s and died in October 1940, shortly after a German air-raid on Wilderness House at Hampton Court, where she was living. Andrei later remarried and lived for many years at Provender, a Kent manor house which was once the hunting lodge of the Black Prince.

Grand Princess Ksenia with her adult children in London in 1923. (*From the left*) Prince Nikita, Prince Vasili, Princess Irina, Prince Rostislav, the Grand Princess, Prince Andrei, Prince Feodor, Prince Dmitri.

Two weddings of the 1920s. (*Right*) Grand Prince Kirill's elder daughter Marie with Prince Karl of Leiningen in 1925. He died in a Soviet labour camp in 1946, a fate shared by several of the German princes. (*Left*) Grand Princess Ksenia's niece and god-daughter Prince Ksenia Georgievna and William Bateman Leeds played together as children but their sudden engagement in 1921, when she was sixteen and he eighteen, shocked the family: 'We all assured them separately, and in concert, that they were far too young even to think of marriage. They only swept aside our objections, and finally threatened to elope and dispense with the marriage ceremony.' The marriage was not a success.

The Dowager Tsaritsa, Maria Feodorovna, photographed shortly before her death in Denmark in October 1928. The last surviving Tsaritsa of Russia and the most loved and respected figure among the exiled community, she was buried in the Danish Cathedral of Roskilde but expressed a wish one day to rest beside her husband Alexander III in the Peter and Paul Cathedral. The ceremony was planned for September 2002, then postponed. It can only be a matter of time.

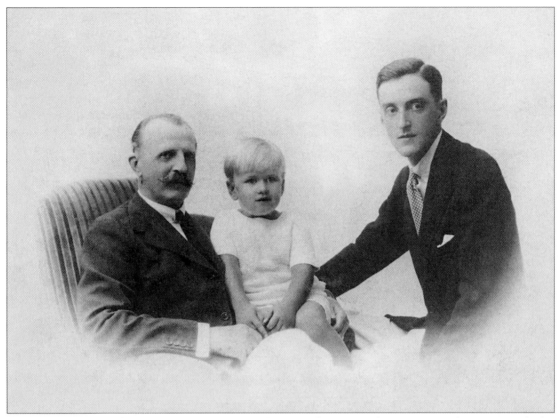

Second only to Maria Feodorovna in the hearts of most exiles was Grand Prince Nikolai Nikolaevich, who commanded immense respect from the men he once led in the field. But he had no children, so the future of the Nikolaevich line lay with his brother Grand Prince Peter, seen here in a classic 'three generations' portrait with his son Prince Roman and grandson Prince Nicholas in about 1924.

Prince Roman married Countess Prascovia Sheremetev at Cap d'Antibes in November 1921 and they had two sons, Nicholas (*right, with the teddy*) and Dimitri. The photo was taken at Cap d'Antibes in 1926.

The effects of war and revolution were traumatic even for those who had long since left Russia and married into other families. Grand Princess Anastasia Mikhailovna, Grand Duchess of Mecklenburg-Schwerin (*left*), had never liked being a German princess and had lived outside her husband's country whenever she could. War with Russia was more than she could bear. Since the French would not allow her, as a German, to live in her villa in Cannes, she spent the war in the Savoy hotel in Lausanne in Switzerland, separated both from her son, the Grand Duke of Mecklenburg-Schwerin, who was with his troops, and from her younger daughter Cecilie, who was married to the German Crown Prince. Anastasia died at Eze, near Cannes, in 1922.

Grand Princess Maria Alexandrovna, Dowager Duchess of Saxe-Coburg, on the other hand, though she was a Tsar's daughter and had always been very Russian in her preferences and her ways, is said to have become ardently pro-German in wartime. But her choice may not have been as simple as it sounds. The Coburg family faced intense hostility on the outbreak of war for their British and Russian connections, none more so than she. Once, driving home from a Red Cross meeting with her younger daughters, her car was held up by a violent crowd shouting insults and abuse. It took an hour for the police to break through and end the ordeal. Under such circumstances a pro-German stance may have been the only one possible. The collapse of the Coburg throne was the final blow and, like her cousins, Maria Alexandrovna took refuge in Switzerland, where she died in October 1920.

Baden, August 1931: Prince Andreas (Andrew) of Greece (*centre*) with his children. The boy in front is his son Prince Philip; the others are (*left to right*) Prince Christoph of Hesse-Cassel and Princess Sophie, Prince Gottfried of Hohenlohe-Langenburg and Princess Margarita, Princess Theodora and Prince Berthold of Baden, Princess Cecile and Hereditary Grand Duke Georg Donatus of Hesse. Queen Olga of Greece had died in exile in Rome in 1926 and Prince Andreas was her fourth son. Her grandson Philip became HRH Prince Philip, Duke of Edinburgh.

Grand Prince Mikhail Mikhailovich with his children, Nadejda (*left*), Mikhail and Anastasia. The Grand Prince spent the war years in England, setting up a hospital in his home, Kenwood House, and supporting war charities. Nadejda married Lord Mountbatten's brother, while her sister became Lady 'Zia' Wehrner. But the Revolution deprived the Grand Prince of his fortune and, despite George V's generosity, he had to accept a much reduced lifestyle. His wife died in 1927 and he visited her grave each day, until his own death less than two years later.

Memories of an even earlier generation of the family endured with Princess Yurievskaya, widow of Alexander II, and her children. The Princess settled in France after her husband's death, leaving her St Petersburg palace for her son's use. He died in 1913 but she lived on until 1922, though the Revolution deprived her of the income promised in her husband's will. Her elder daughter Olga (*below right*) married Count Georg Merenberg, a morganatic cousin of the Nassaus (the reigning family of Luxembourg) and lived in Germany. The younger, Catherine (*below left*), married a Russian, Prince Bariatinsky, but was widowed in 1910. She remarried in Yalta in 1916 and, after a hair-raising escape overland from the Crimea two years later, tried to make her way as an opera singer. She died on Hayling Island in 1959, lonely and impoverished but surrounded still by an intangible air of the past.

In recent years documentary evidence about the imperial family in the nineteenth and early twentieth centuries has started to emerge from Russia where, against all expectation, most of the archival material has been preserved. This should improve our understanding of events which for decades have come to us principally through the memoirs of the exiles. There was a spate of these books in the 1920s and 1930s, mostly written by courtiers, though several members of the imperial family also had their say. Maria Pavlovna the younger (*above left*) wrote *Things I Have Known* and *A Princess in Exile*, giving valuable though rather slanted accounts of her upbringing and later career. The most influential autobiography of all, Alexander Mikhailovich's *Once a Grand Duke* (*above right*) is a colourful book, shaped by the author's need to tell a good story on the American lecture circuit, but it is full of inaccuracies. Its vicious attacks on other members of the imperial family have dominated later interpretations of them. Prince Gavril Konstantinovich (*right*) also wrote memoirs, but his *In the Marble Palace* has only been published in Russian.

(*Above*) As documents emerge, so too do the physical reminders of imperial Russia. The Alexander Palace, which was home to Nicholas I and his family, to Alexander III before he became Tsar, and to the family of Nicholas II, is becoming accessible again after decades in the hands of the Navy Department. Since this photograph was taken, the wing on the left, which houses the private rooms of the last Tsar's family, has been repainted on the outside and opened as a museum – still in its early stages, it is developing all the time.

(*Above*) The only memorial to Nicholas II in Russia stands on open ground behind the Feodorovsky Cathedral, a few minutes walk from the Alexander Palace. The Cathedral was completed in 1912 for the use of the Combined Regiment of the Guards and it became a special church to the Tsar and Tsaritsa and their children, and their most regular place of worship in the final years. Cut flowers are left regularly at the foot of the memorial, beside the carefully tended garden.

(*Left*) This monument to the Tsesarevich Alexei was unveiled outside the Cottage at Alexandria Peterhof in August 1994, on what would have been his ninetieth birthday.

Moscow too is relearning its memories, particularly of the couple who once cared so much for the city. In 1995 the coffin of the murdered Grand Prince Sergei Alexandrovich was carried with great reverence to the Novospassky Monastery for reburial. It had been discovered five years earlier in a blocked-up vault under a Kremlin car park. Until the Revolution a memorial cross bearing the words 'Father, forgive them, for they know not what they do', designed by Victor Vasnetsov, marked the place where Sergei died; a replica has been set up in the monastery grounds (*above*). The serene statue (*right*) of his wife Grand Princess Elizaveta Feodorovna was the first of the new memorials and stands in the garden of her Martha and Mary Convent. This is once again a living institution, where the nuns strive to rebuild the work started by Elizaveta and to restore the physical surroundings she created. In April 1992 the Patriarch celebrated her canonisation as a saint of the Orthodox church, and proceedings are underway for the canonisation of her husband.

This, to western eyes, is the strangest image of all: an icon of the last Tsar and his family sold as a focus for prayer in an ordinary church in Russia where, not so many years ago, even to mention them in kindness could earn harsh punishment. There is no shortage of 'imperial' souvenirs designed for the tourists in today's Russia, but the icons belong to something different: a genuine upsurge of emotion – part reverence, part regret, part sorrow – for the past and all its victims, drawn to a head in the story of the last Tsar. Not everyone feels it. The canonisation of the imperial family in August 2000 was controversial, and many people still blame Nicholas II for everything Russia has suffered. Most are indifferent. But the feeling does exist and is discernible particularly in places once associated with the imperial family. Beyond this, an ever-growing catalogue of exhibitions and publications about the family in Russian (*below*) bears witness at least to curiosity about the family, whose lives were a forbidden subject for decades.

Family Trees

Almost all members and descendants of the imperial family who feature in this book can be found somewhere on the family trees:

Tree 1 shows the last three Tsars, Alexander II, Alexander III and Nicholas II and their descendants;

Tree 2 'The Descendants of Nicholas I' shows the Konstantinovich, Nikolaevich and Mikhailovich branches of the imperial family;

Tree 3 'The Descendants of Tsar Paul' illustrates the more remote connections featured in Chapter 7.

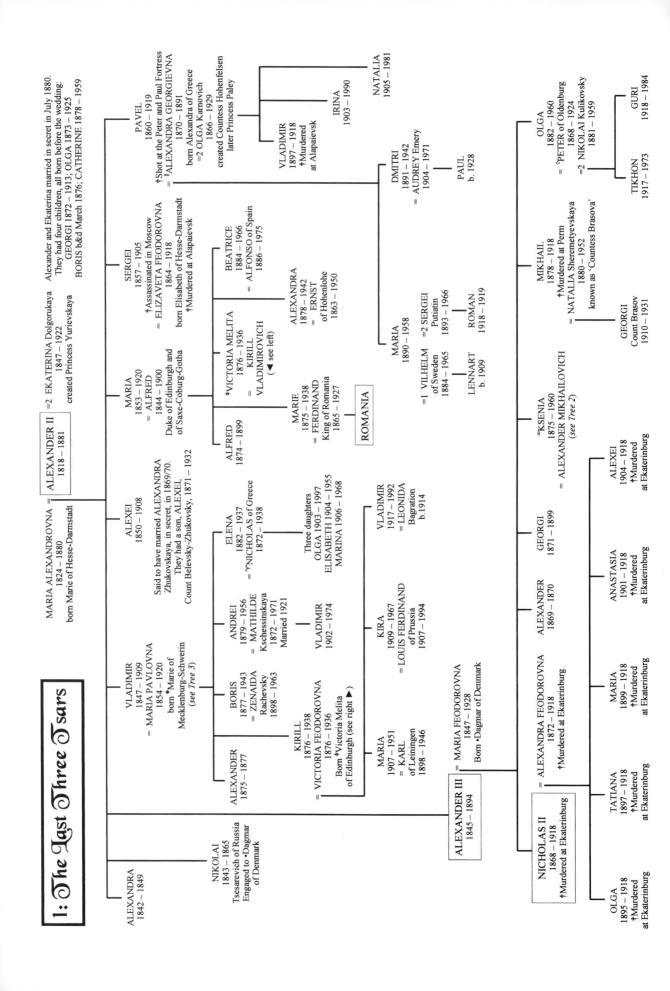

1: The Last Three Tsars

MARIA ALEXANDROVNA = ALEXANDER II =2 EKATERINA Dolgorukaya
1824 – 1880   1818 – 1881   1847 – 1922
born Marie of Hesse-Darmstadt   created Princess Yurievskaya

Alexander and Ekaterina married in secret in July 1880.
They had four children, all born before the wedding:
GEORGI 1872 – 1913; OLGA 1873 – 1925
BORIS b&d March 1876; CATHERINE 1878 – 1959

ALEXANDRA
1842 – 1849

NIKOLAI
1843 – 1865
Tsesarevich of Russia
Engaged to •Dagmar
of Denmark

VLADIMIR
1847 – 1909
= MARIA PAVLOVNA
1854 – 1920
born •Marie of
Mecklenburg-Schwerin
(see Tree 3)

ALEXANDER
1875 – 1877

KIRILL
1876 – 1938
= VICTORIA FEODOROVNA
1876 – 1936
Born •Victoria Melita
of Edinburgh (see right ▶)

MARIA
1907 – 1951
= KARL
of Leiningen
1898 – 1946

BORIS
1877 – 1943
= ZENAIDA
Rachevsky
1898 – 1963

ANDREI
1879 – 1956
= MATHILDE
Kschessinskaya
1872 – 1971
Married 1921

VLADIMIR
1902 – 1974

ELENA
1882 – 1937
= ᵞNICHOLAS of Greece
1872 – 1938

Three daughters
OLGA 1903 – 1997
ELISABETH 1904 – 1955
MARINA 1906 – 1968

KIRA
1909 – 1967
= LOUIS FERDINAND
of Prussia
1907 – 1994

VLADIMIR
1917 – 1992
= LEONIDA
Bagration
b.1914

ALEXEI
1850 – 1908

Said to have married ALEXANDRA
Zhukovskaya, in secret, in 1869/70.
They had a son, ALEXEI,
Count Belevsky-Zhukovsky, 1871 – 1932

MARIA
1853 – 1920
= ALFRED
1844 – 1900
Duke of Edinburgh and
of Saxe-Coburg-Gotha

ALFRED
1874 – 1899

MARIE
1875 – 1938
= FERDINAND
King of Romania
1865 – 1927

ROMANIA

ᵠVICTORIA MELITA
1876 – 1936
= KIRILL
VLADIMIROVICH
(◀ see left)

BEATRICE
1884 – 1966
= ALFONSO of Spain
1886 – 1975

ALEXANDRA
1878 – 1942
= ERNST
of Hohenlohe
1863 – 1950

SERGEI
1857 – 1905
†Assassinated in Moscow
= ELIZAVETA FEODOROVNA
1864 – 1918
born Elisabeth of Hesse-Darmstadt
†Murdered at Alapaievsk

PAVEL
1860 – 1919
†Shot at the Peter and Paul Fortress
= §ALEXANDRA GEORGIEVNA
1870 – 1891
born Alexandra of Greece
=2 OLGA Karnovich
1866 – 1929
created Countess Hohenfelsen
later Princess Paley

VLADIMIR
1897 – 1918
†Murdered
at Alapaievsk

IRINA
1903 – 1990

NATALIA
1905 – 1981

DMITRI
1891 – 1942
= AUDREY Emery
1904 – 1971

PAUL
b. 1928

MARIA
1890 – 1958
=1 VILHELM
of Sweden
1884 – 1965

LENNART
b. 1909

=2 SERGEI
Putiatin
1893 – 1966

ROMAN
1918 – 1919

= MARIA FEODOROVNA
1847 – 1928
Born •Dagmar of Denmark

ALEXANDER III
1845 – 1894

= ALEXANDRA FEODOROVNA
1872 – 1918
†Murdered at Ekaterinburg

NICHOLAS II
1868 – 1918
†Murdered at Ekaterinburg

OLGA
1895 – 1918
†Murdered
at Ekaterinburg

TATIANA
1897 – 1918
†Murdered
at Ekaterinburg

MARIA
1899 – 1918
†Murdered
at Ekaterinburg

ANASTASIA
1901 – 1918
†Murdered
at Ekaterinburg

ALEXEI
1904 – 1918
†Murdered
at Ekaterinburg

ALEXANDER
1869 – 1870

GEORGI
1871 – 1899

∞KSENIA
1875 – 1960
= ALEXANDER MIKHAILOVICH
(see Tree 2)

MIKHAIL
1878 – 1918
†Murdered at Perm
= NATALIA Sheremetyevskaya
1880 – 1952
known as 'Countess Brasova'

GEORGI
Count Brasov
1910 – 1931

OLGA
1882 – 1960
= ⁰PETER of Oldenburg
1868 – 1924
=2 NIKOLAI Kulikovsky
1881 – 1959

TIKHON
1917 – 1973

GURI
1918 – 1984

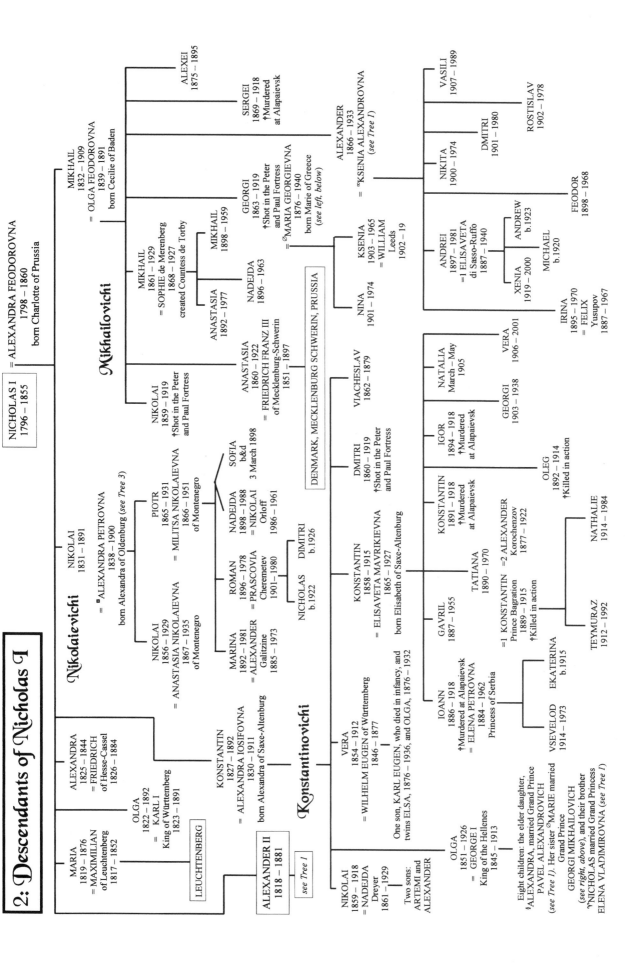

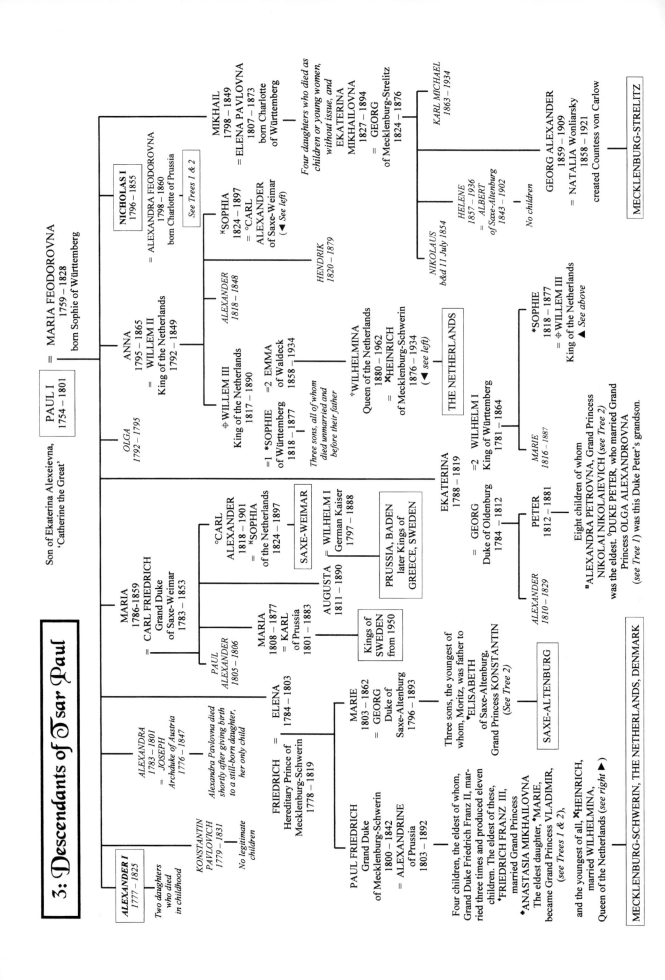

3: Descendants of Tsar Paul

PAUL I
1754 – 1801

Son of Ekaterina Alexeievna,
'Catherine the Great'

= MARIA FEODOROVNA
1759 – 1828
born Sophie of Württemberg

ALEXANDER I
1777 – 1825

*Two daughters
who died
in childhood*

*KONSTANTIN
PAVLOVICH*
1779 – 1831

*No legitimate
children*

ALEXANDRA
1783 – 1801
*= JOSEPH
Archduke of Austria
1776 – 1847*

*Alexandra Pavlovna died
shortly after giving birth
to a still-born daughter,
her only child*

MARIA
1786-1859
= CARL FRIEDRICH
Grand Duke of Saxe-Weimar
1783 – 1853

*PAUL
ALEXANDER*
1805 – 1806

MARIA
1808 – 1877
= KARL
of Prussia
1801 – 1883

**Kings of SWEDEN
from 1950**

°CARL
ALEXANDER
1818 – 1901
= *SOPHIE
of the Netherlands
1824 – 1897

SAXE-WEIMAR

AUGUSTA
1811 – 1890
= WILHELM I
German Kaiser
1797 – 1888

**PRUSSIA, BADEN
later Kings of
GREECE, SWEDEN**

OLGA
1792 – 1795

ANNA
1795 – 1865
= WILLEM II
King of the Netherlands
1792 – 1849

⊕ WILLEM III
King of the Netherlands
1817 – 1890
=1 *SOPHIE
of Württemberg
1818 – 1877
=2 EMMA
of Waldeck
1858 – 1934

*Three sons, all of whom
died unmarried and
before their father*

ALEXANDER
1818 – 1848

HENDRIK
1820 – 1879

*WILHELMINA
Queen of the Netherlands
1880 – 1962
= ✕HEINRICH
of Mecklenburg-Schwerin
1876 – 1934
(▼ see left)

THE NETHERLANDS

NICHOLAS I
1796 – 1855
= ALEXANDRA FEODOROVNA
1798 – 1860
born Charlotte of Prussia

See Trees 1 & 2

*SOPHIA
1824 – 1897
= °CARL
ALEXANDER of Saxe-Weimar
(▼ See left)

MIKHAIL
1798 – 1849
= ELENA PAVLOVNA
1807 – 1873
born Charlotte
of Württemberg

*Four daughters who died as
children or young women,
without issue, and
EKATERINA
MIKHAILOVNA
1827 – 1894
= GEORG
of Mecklenburg-Strelitz
1824 – 1876

KARL MICHAEL
1863 – 1934

*HELENE
1857 – 1936
of Saxe-Altenburg
= ALBERT
1843 – 1902

No children

*NIKOLAUS
b&d 11 July 1854*

GEORG ALEXANDER
1859 – 1909
= NATALIA Wonliarsky
1858 – 1921
created Countess von Carlow

MECKLENBURG-STRELITZ

FRIEDRICH
Hereditary Prince of
Mecklenburg-Schwerin
1778 – 1819
= ELENA
1784 – 1803

PAUL FRIEDRICH
Grand Duke
of Mecklenburg-Schwerin
1800 – 1842
= ALEXANDRINE
of Prussia
1803 – 1892

MARIE
1803 – 1862
= GEORG
Duke of
Saxe-Altenburg
1796 – 1893

*Three sons, the youngest of
whom, Moritz, was father to
♦ELISABETH
of Saxe-Altenburg,
Grand Princess KONSTANTIN
(See Tree 2)*

SAXE-ALTENBURG

Four children, the eldest of whom,
Grand Duke Friedrich Franz II, married three times and produced eleven
children. The eldest of these,
♦FRIEDRICH FRANZ III,
married Grand Princess
♦ANASTASIA MIKHAILOVNA
The eldest daughter, ♦MARIE,
became Grand Princess VLADIMIR,
(see Trees 1 & 2),
and the youngest of all, ✕HEINRICH,
married WILHELMINA (see right ▼),
Queen of the Netherlands (see right ▲)

MECKLENBURG-SCHWERIN, THE NETHERLANDS, DENMARK

EKATERINA
1788 – 1819
=1 GEORG
Duke of Oldenburg
1784 – 1812
=2 WILHELM I
King of Württemberg
1781 – 1864

ALEXANDER
1810 – 1829

PETER
1812 – 1881

MARIE
1816 – 1887

Eight children of whom
¤ALEXANDRA PETROVNA, Grand Princess
NIKOLAI NIKOLAIEVICH (see Tree 2)
was the eldest. °DUKE PETER, who married Grand
Princess OLGA ALEXANDROVNA
(see Tree 1) was this Duke Peter's grandson.

*SOPHIE
1818 – 1877
= ⊕ WILLEM III
King of the Netherlands
▲ See above

Notes

There appears to be only one book in English on photography in Russia, David Elliott's *Photography in Russia, 1840–1940* (London, Thames & Hudson, 1992). Books on the imperial family are legion. Sadly, some of the most interesting and challenging documentary material is appearing in exhibition catalogues which are, by their very nature, ephemeral and difficult to track down. But at least it is appearing . . .

Introduction
1. E.M. Almedingen, *The Emperor Alexander II* (Bodley Head, 1962), p. 137
2. The first actual photograph is reckoned to be Joseph Niépce's view of the courtyard and rooftops of his house at Chalon-sur-Saône, taken in 1826 on a chemically treated pewter plate, but since this required an exposure time of eight hours the method was not practicable. Niépce entered into partnership with Daguerre in 1829 and the two worked together until Niépce's death in 1833
3. Quoted in Elena Barkhatova, "The First Photographs in Russia", David Elliott, *Photography in Russia, 1840–1940* (Thames & Hudson 1992), p. 26
4. Quoted in David Elliott, 'The Photograph in Russia: icon of a new age', David Elliott, *Photography in Russia, 1840–1940* (Thames & Hudson, 1992), p. 13
5. Quoted in Gannardy Belovalov, 'Dostoevsky and the Imperial Family', *Maria Feodorovna, Empress of Russia* (Exhibition Catalogue, Christiansborg Palace, Copenhagen, 1997), p. 270
6. Quoted in A.I. Barkovets, 'Emperor Nicholas II – The Freezing of a Moment'; Photographs of the last imperial family held in the stores of the State Archives of the Russian Federation, *Nicholas II: The Family Album* (Exhibition Catalogue, Moscow, 1998), p. 27

Chapter 1 – The Last Tsar
p. 3 'I recognised . . . me', E. Fricero, *Nicolas Alexandrovich* (Nice, Meyerbeer, 1951) p. 2 (author's translation)
'I cannot . . . so far', quoted in 'Nixa, Minny and Sacha' by Aliya Barkovetz in *Maria Feodorovna*, p. 74
'I don't . . . done', ibid, p. 84
p. 4 'before . . . his proposal', quoted in 'The Empress Maria Feodorovna in Memoirs of Russian Political and Public Figures' by Andrey D. Yanovsky in *Maria Feodorovna*, p. 240
p. 6 'cheerful . . . sunset', Alexander, Grand Duke of Russia, *Once a Grand Duke* (New York, Farrar & Rinehart, 1932), p. 24
p. 8 'He looked . . . indoors', *The Graphic*, 24 May 1884, p. 512
'Alix and I . . . Ernie', quoted in Andrei Maylunas and Sergei Mironenko, *A Lifelong Passion* (London, Weidenfeld & Nicolson, 1996), pp. 10, 11 (entries written on two successive days)
p. 9 'Aliicé . . . spoilt', Princess Alice, *Alice, Princess of Great Britain, Grand Duchess of Hesse, Letters to Her Majesty The Queen* (London, John Murray, 1897), p. 209
p. 10 'the ice . . . pink flowers', quoted in *A Lifelong Passion*, p. 16
p. 11 'I've noticed . . . surprising thing', quoted in *Nicholas and Alexandra; The Last Imperial Family of Tsarist Russia*, Exhibition Catalogue (Booth-Clibborn Editions, 1998), p. 270
'While I was . . . happen', quoted in *A Lifelong Passion*, p. 22
p. 12 'I was so happy . . . child', ibid, p. 50
p. 14 'Our little . . . feed her', ibid, p. 166
p. 15 'She was . . . possible', M. Eagar, *Six Years at the Russian Court* (London, Hurst & Blackett, 1906), p. 38
p. 16 'My God! . . . girl' and 'Forgive us . . . daughter', both quoted in *A Lifelong Passion*, p. 206
'every man . . . mentioned', Baroness Sophie Buxhoeveden, *Before the Storm* (London, Macmillan, 1938), p. 237
p. 17 'all dressed . . . animal' and 'Little Marie . . . the nurse', ibid, p. 246
p. 18 'It would . . . infectious', Pierre Gilliard, *Thirteen Years at the Russian Court* (London, Hutchinson, nd), pp. 74–6
p. 20 'He had . . . the future', quoted in *Nicholas II; the Imperial Family* (Abris Publishers, St Petersburg, 1998),

pp. 105–6 – with slight rephrasing to ease an awkward translation

Chapter 2 – The Family

p. 25 'a boy . . . his elders', Marie, Princess of Battenberg, *Reminiscences* (London, Allen & Unwin, 1925), pp. 5–6
p. 28 'When you . . . take over', A.F. Tiutcheva, *Pre Dvore Dvuch Imperatorov* (Moscow, Muisl, 1990), p. 103 (author's translation)
'My little Puss-in-Boots', Countess Kleinmichel, *Memories of a Shipwrecked World* (London, Brentano's, 1923), p. 151
p. 29 'No doubt . . . duty', Podewils, Gräfin Sophie Dorothee (ed.), *Traum der Jugend goldner Stern; Aus Der Aufzeichningen Der Königin Olga von Württemberg* (Reutlingen, Günther Neske, 1955), pp. 90–1
p. 36 'authoritarian republicanism', quoted in Preben Ulstrup, 'The Danish Royal Family and the Russian Imperial Family', in *Treasures of Russia – Imperial Gifts* (Copenhagen, Amalienborg Palace Exhibition Catalogue, 2002), p. 160
p. 38 'one of my best . . . laughter', Grand Duchess George, *A Romanov Diary* (New York, Atlantic International Publications, 1988), p. 83

Chapter 3 – Marrying into the Family

p. 40 'that for the . . . to a soul', W.A.L. Seaman (ed.), *The Russian Journal of Lady Londonderry* (London, John Murray, 1973), p. 132
'one must agree . . . frightful', quoted in S.W. Jackman (ed.), *Romanov Relations* (London, Macmillan, 1969), p. 21: Grand Prince Konstantin Pavlovich to their sister Anna.
p. 41 'This was Marie . . . meeting', *Traum der Jugend*, p. 142
'I don't know . . . in love', quoted in Olga Barkowez, Fjodor Federow and Alexander Krylow, *Peterhof ist ein Traum; Deutsche Prinzessinnen in Russland* (Berlin, Quintessenz Verlags, 2001), p. 78
'she takes . . . jolly pranks', ibid, p. 101
p. 42 'I have prayed . . . this day', ibid, p. 56
'very good-humoured . . . love him', quoted in Roger Fulford (ed.), *Dearest Child* (London, Evans Brothers, 1964), pp. 274–5: letter to the Crown Princess of Prussia, 24 October 1860
'a creature of gold . . .', quoted in Preben Ulstrup, 'The Danish Royal Family and the Russian Imperial Family', p. 159
'an unusually clever . . . from her', Elizabeth Narishkin-Kurakin, *Under Three Tsars* (New York, Dutton, 1931), p. 95
p. 46 'I promise you . . . I love you', quoted in *Peterhof ist ein Traum*, p. 123
'After the words . . . my heart', ibid, p. 125

'she belongs to us . . .', ibid, p. 128
p. 47 'I did not hesitate . . . happy', quoted by Alexander Bokhanov in 'Ella and Sergei', *Royalty*, vol. 12, no. 11, p. 60
'He was often . . . secrecy', Ernst Ludwig, Großherzog von Hessen und bei Rhein, *Erinnertes* (Darmstadt, Eduard Roether, 1983), p. 76
'Sergei is . . . for him', quoted by Hugo Mager in *Elizabeth, Grand Duchess of Russia* (New York, Carrol & Graf, 1998), p. 99
p. 48 'People will intrigue . . . calumniated', quoted by Lubov Millar in *Grand Duchess Elizabeth* (Redding, California, Nicodemus Publication Society, 1991), p. 92
'He was a real angel . . . complain', ibid, p. 63
'Poor Sergei . . . blessing', quoted by Bokhanov, 'Ella and Sergei', p. 64
p. 49 'The newly-weds . . . Feodorovna', Alexei Volkov, *Souvenirs d'Alexis Volkov: Valet de Chambre de la Tsarine Alexandra Feodorovna* (Paris, Payot, 1928) – author's translation
p. 52 'She seemed touched . . . married life', Baroness de Stoeckl, *Not all Vanity* (London, John Murray, 1950), p. 142
p. 56 'A famous beauty . . . moment', *Before the Storm*, p. 219

Chapter 4 – Born Romanov

p. 57 'On 8 September . . . in her arms', *Traum der Jugend*, pp. 198–9. The year was 1843
p. 58 ''What a joy . . . like a baby', quoted in *The Romanovs; Love, Power and Tragedy* (London, Leppi Publications, 1993), p. 18
p. 59 'Then he moved . . . days ago', E.M. Almedingen, *An Unbroken Unity* (London, Bodley Head, 1964), p. 87
p. 60 'Baby is growing . . . floor', quoted in *A Lifelong Passion*, p. 152
'Our little ones . . . in their arms', ibid, p. 315
p. 61 'The one amusing . . . that', ibid, p. 162
'Days before . . . gifts', Grand Duchess Marie of Russia, *Things I Remember* (London, Cassell, 1930), p. 12
p. 62 'At first . . . Velikii Kniaz', quoted in *Peterhof ist ein Traum*, p. 132 (author's translation)
p. 63 'Little Micha . . . own way', quoted in 'Our Beloved Empress' by Yulia V. Kudrina in *Maria Feodorovna*, p. 39
'Before tea . . . sweet with us', quoted in *A Lifelong Passion*, p. 154
p. 65 'Milly was with us . . . Oliver Twist', HIH the Grand Duke Cyril, *My Life in Russia's Service – Then and Now* (London, Selwyn & Blount, 1939), p. 13
p. 66 'She was always . . . in exile', Prince Roman Romanow, *Am Hof des Letzten Zaren* (Munich and Zurich, Piper, 1991), p. 28 (author's translation)

p. 67 'The cossacks . . . corridor', quoted in *A Lifelong Passion*, p. 166

'he was in some trouble . . . troubles', *Six Years at the Russian Court*, p. 120

p. 68 'Her appearance in our midst . . . embrace', Marie, Queen of Romania, *The Story of My Life* (London, Cassell, 1934), vol. I, pp. 102–3

p. 69 'It was characteristic . . . permission', Crown Princess Cecilie, *Memoirs* (London, Gollancz, 1931), p. 26

p. 71 'and the Queen . . . to kiss', *Am Hof des Letzten Zaren*, p. 37 (author's translation)

Chapter 5 – The Training of Princes

p. 76 'The Heir . . . great skill', *Pre Dvore Dvuch Imperatorov*, p. 156

'Dearest Mama . . . and all of you', Tsesarevich Nikolai to Tsaritsa Maria Alexandrovna, 14/26 August 1857; private collection. 'Seriozha' was a pet name for baby Sergei and 'Seichik' for Alexei. 'Mary' was their sister Marie

p. 78 'an English gentleman . . . manly', W.T. Stead, 'Nicholas II, Czar of Russia and "Emperor of Peace"' in *Review of Reviews*, 1899, p. 45

'If you do not come . . . Come quickly', quoted in Coryne Hall, 'Dear Siocha; A Swiss at the Russian Court' in *Royalty Digest*, vol. XII, no. 4, pp. 98–102, on which this paragraph is based

p. 79 'Famous archaeologists . . . the empire', *Before the Storm*, pp. 223–4

p. 84 'The officer's dress . . . uniforms', Alexander II and Grand Prince Konstantin Nikolaevich, *1857–1961; Peesma, Dnevniki* (Moscow, Terra, 1994), p. 17 (author's translation)

p. 85 'I can honestly say . . . indifferent', quoted in *Jewels of the Romanovs* (Exhibition catalogue, The American-Russian Cultural Cooperation Foundation, 1997), p. 13

'an enchanting companion . . . conversible', The Dean of Windsor and Hector Bolitho (eds), *Later Letters of Lady Augusta Stanley 1864–1876* (London, Jonathan Cape, 1929), p. 217

p. 86 'How clearly . . . in jail', *Once a Grand Duke*, pp. 81–2

'before anything could be done . . . spoken', *My Life in Russia's Service*, p. 39

p. 87 'I am now happier . . . camp life', Edward J. Bing (ed.), *The Letters of Tsar Nicholas and Empress Marie* (London, Nicholson & Watson, 1937), p. 33

'before all my thoughts . . . burden', quoted in *A Lifelong Passion*, p. 123

p. 88 'Believe in God . . . men', Alexandre Spiridovich, *Les Dernières Années de la Cour de Tzarskoie-Sélo* (Paris, Payot, 1928), pp. 182–3

'From the age of seven . . . sword', Prince Gavril Konstantinovich, *In the Marble Palace* (Zakharov, Moscow, 2001), pp. 51–2

p. 89 'a friend . . . decisions', *Later Letters of Lady Augusta Stanley*, p. 204

'As a child . . . of her own', *A Romanov Diary*, p. 111

p. 90 'suddenly she seized . . . fury', H. Jones Thaddeus, *Recollections of a Court Painter* (London, The Bodley Head, 1912), pp. 112–13

'Poor little thing . . . grandiose', quoted in Preben Ulstrup, 'The Danish Royal Family and the Russian Imperial Family', p. 121

p. 91 'Delightful fair-haired little girls . . . procession passed', *Before the Storm*, p. 240

Chapter 6 – A Suitable Marriage

p. 94 'We lost . . . our walks', *Later Letters of Lady Augusta Stanley*, p. 218; these are Alexander II's words at the time of his daughter's wedding, as reported by Lady Stanley

p. 95 'Where in the world . . . this kind', quoted in 'Our Beloved Empress' by Yulia V. Kudrina in *Maria Feodorovna*, p. 44

p. 97 'he has a rather revolting illness . . . marry', quoted in Preben Ulstrup, 'The Danish Royal Family and the Russian Imperial Family', p. 162

'You can . . . Mecklenburg', quoted in *Peterhof ist ein Traum*, p. 210

'so sweet . . . to bury', quoted in Preben Ulstrup, 'The Danish Royal Family and the Russian Imperial Family', p. 162

'the dearest man on earth', Daisy, Princess of Pless, *From My Private Diary* (London, John Murray, 1931), p. 93

p. 99 'Their upbringing . . . shock people', quoted in Preben Ulstrup, 'The Danish Royal Family and the Russian Imperial Family', p. 121

p. 100 'My Dearest . . . my eyes', 'You make . . . with love', quoted in Patricia Phenix, *Olga Romanov; Russia's Last Grand Duchess* (Canada, Viking, 1999), pp. 59, 60

p. 101 'her haste . . . compact', *Things I Remember*, pp. 93, 97

'She was full of life . . . to deal with', *A Romanov Diary*, p. 133

'and to live . . . last letters', quoted in Marion Meinert, *Großfürstin Maria; Schicksal einer Romanoff* (Switzerland; undated exhibition catalogue from Schloss Mainau, printed by Druckerei Konstanz), 9th page

p. 102 'Did you hear . . . social era', Maria Alexandrovna, Duchess of Saxe-Coburg-Gotha, to the Crown Princess of Romania, 24 May 1911; copy in private hands

p. 103 'The young Kostia . . . telegraph to me', the same to the same, 17 October 1911; copy in private hands

p. 104 'My dear boy . . . no one else', quoted in Edvard Radzinsky, *Rasputin; The Last Word* (London, Weidenfeld & Nicolson, 2000), p. 196

p. 105 'He has completely lost . . . demanded', quoted in Preben Ulstrup, 'The Danish Royal Family and the Russian Imperial Family', p. 146

p. 108 'He was exceptionally good-looking . . . long time', Mathilde Kschessinska, *Dancing in Petersburg* (London, Doubleday, 1961), p. 78

'knew for certain . . . forgave me everything', ibid, p. 89

p. 109 'I . . . might never have decided . . . happen', quoted in Rosemary and Donald Crawford, *Michael & Natasha* (London, Weidenfeld & Nicolson, 1997), p. 130

p. 110 'God grant him good fortune . . . distressing', quoted by O. Barkovets in 'Moe S. . .', in *Sred shumnovo bala* (Moscow, Exhibition Catalogue, GARF, 2001), p. 53

Chapter 7 – Family Ties

p. 112 'Here at last . . . state', 'Nicholas II, Czar of Russia and "Emperor of Peace"', p. 43

'I had . . . conflict', H.R.H. Wilhelmina, Princess of the Netherlands, *Lonely But Not Alone* (London, Hutchinson, 1959), p. 70

p. 117 'Dear children . . . tell you', *Traum der Jugend*, p. 11

p. 121 (*above*) Some believe that the woman on the left is Marie, Princess Valdemar of Denmark; really it could be either.

p. 122 'My evening . . . ME', quoted in *The Romanovs; Love, Power and Tragedy*, p. 28. The separate sentences were from different entries in the diary

p. 124 'She often . . . kept', *Six Years at the Russian Court*, p. 144

p. 125, below. The 1903 wedding group shows: (*in front, left to right*) Grand Duke Ernst Ludwig of Hesse; Nicholas of Greece and Elena Vladimirovna; Prince George of Battenberg; Tatiana Nikolaevna; Elisabeth of Hesse (Ernst Ludwig's daughter by Victoria Melita, who died a few weeks after this was taken, while on a visit to her Russian cousins); Olga Nikolaevna; Anastasia and Marie Nikolaevna, with their mother the Tsaritsa; Elizaveta Feodorovna, George of Greece. (*Behind, from top left*) Prince Heinrich of Prussia and Princess Irène; Victoria, Princess Louis of Battenberg; Marie, Princess of Erbach-Schönberg; Sergei Alexandrovich; Queen Olga of Greece in front of Alexandra, Princess of Wales; Maria Pavlovna the younger; Vera of Württemberg (dark hat); King George of the Hellenes: Dmitri Pavlovich (small boy) in front of Prince Friedrich Carl of Hesse-Cassel; Prince Christopher of Greece (bigger boy); Princess Louise of Battenberg (in front of him, looking down); Georgi Mikhailovich (dark suit) and Maria Georgievna; the Tsar Crown Prince Constantine obscuring Princess Victoria of Wales; Sophie, Crown Princess of Greece; Margarete, Princess Friedrich Karl

p. 132 For further details about the foundation of the Martha and Mary Convent, see *An Unbroken Unity*

Chapter 8 – The Family at Work

p. 137 'he was . . . Serge', quoted in Lubov Millar, *Grand Duchess Elizabeth* (Redding, California, Nicodemus Publication Society, 1991), pp. 67–8

'Since . . . localities,' Kaiser Wilhelm II, *My Early Life* (London, Methuen, 1926), p. 320

p. 138 'He is . . . the first,' quoted in *A Lifelong Passion*, p. 103

'I think . . . the young,' ibid, p. 173

p. 139 'He could . . . us', Alexandre Spiridovich, *Les Dernières Années de la Cour de Tzarskoié-Sélo* (Paris, Payot, 1928), p. 386

p. 145 'exceedingly . . . hoar-frost', *The Story of My Life*, vol. II, p. 79

p. 147 'She was . . . marching', Baroness Sophie Buxhoeveden, *The Life & Tragedy of Alexandra Feodorovna* (London, Longmans, 1928), p. 81

Chapter 9 – The Family at Play

p. 154 'While she was . . . Marina's talent', *Am Hof des Letzten Zaren*, p. 148

p. 155 'to my much loved son Nicholas', *Peterhof ist ein Traum*, p. 75

p. 156 'It was a moving . . . true poet', *Before the Storm*, p. 225

p. 157 'with great feeling . . . once again', *Am Hof des Letzten Zaren*, p. 62

p. 167 'If it's true . . . Grand Duke', *A Lifelong Passion*, p. 167

p. 169 'There was something . . . stay for ever', *Once a Grand Duke*, p. 204

p. 172 'He stood on the top deck . . . with tears', *Not All Vanity*, pp. 119–20

Chapter 10 – The Passing of Tsars

p. 176 'She could not . . . recover', *Am Hof des Letzten Zaren*, p. 145

p. 177 'Whatever there is . . . faith', *Peterhof ist ein Traum*, p. 41

p. 178 'The doctors . . . of him', quoted in Preben Ulstrup, 'The Danish Royal Family and the Russian Imperial Family', pp. 105–6

'So we never . . . 10th', *Kniaz Oleg* (St Petersburg, 1915, reprinted by Kazan, Star, 1995), p. 43

p. 179 'collapsed one day . . . suffering', *Souvenirs d'Alexis Volkov*

'The doctors . . . niece', ibid

p. 180 'This was . . . earth', quoted in E. Fricero, *Nicolas Alexandrovich*, p. 15

p. 182 'Slava lay . . . so soon' and 'Slava so loved . . . ceremonial', quoted in Mikhail Vostruishev, *Avgustieshii Semiestvo; Rossia glazami Velikovo Kniazia Konstantina Konstantinovicha* (Moscow, Olma-Press, 2001), p. 177

'A brilliant boy . . . sincerity', *Once a Grand Duke*, p. 24

'The first time . . . coffin', *My Life in Russia's Service*, p. 54

p. 184 The most recent version of the story appears in *White Crow; the Life and Times of the Grand Duke Nicholas Mikhailovich Romanov*, by Jamie Cockfield (Westport Connecticut, Praeger, 2002); some interesting documents are quoted by Preben Ulstrup in 'The Danish Royal Family and the Russian Imperial Family'

p. 185 'My father . . . last wish', quoted in Olga Barkovets, 'The Reformer's Dismissal', in *Grand Duke Konstantin Nikolayevich* (St Petersburg, Abris Art Publishers, 2002), p. 51 (with minor alterations to smooth an awkward translation)

'sitting . . . was over', Prince Gavril Konstantinovich, *V Mramornom Dvortse; Memuari* (Moscow, Zaharov, 2001), p. 271

p. 186 Details of the funeral, and of the box, are taken from *V Mramornom Dvortse*, p. 274

p. 188 'I felt . . . and loved', Olga Voronov, *Upheaval* (London, Hutchinson, nd), p. 67

'every day . . . interruption', quoted in *A Lifelong Passion*, p. 267; the words are those of the Grand Prince's ADC

'the ribbon . . . before', *Upheaval*, pp. 67–8

p. 189 'May God . . . my eyes', quoted in *A Lifelong Passion*, p. 272

Chapter 11 – War and Revolution

p. 193 'a thorough . . . sympathy', *Under Three Tsars*, p. 50

p. 194 'Where the . . . impression', *My Life in Russia's Service*, p. 171

p. 195 'Words could not express . . . it would remain', *Am Hof des Letzten Zaren*, p. 112

p. 197 'I am . . . its blood', Olga Novikoff, *Russian Memories* (London, Herbert Jenkins, 1917), p. 261

p. 198 'To some . . . is useful', *The Life & Tragedy of Alexandra Feodorovna*, p. 192

p. 199 'How charming . . . soldiers' and 'that the dog . . . he', *A Lifelong Passion*, p. 442

p. 201 'It was . . . trouble', *The Russian Diary of an Englishman* (London, Heinemann, 1919), p. 33

'In reviewing . . . noble work', quoted in Marion Wynn, 'Another Royal visitor to Harrogate', *Royalty Digest*, vol. XI, no. 3, p. 82

p. 204 'Nothing . . . two years', quoted in Preben Ulstrup, 'The Danish Royal Family and the Russian Imperial Family', p. 120

'An inexperienced . . . more', Joseph T. Fuhrmann (ed.), *The Complete Wartime Correspondence of Tsar Nicholas II and the Empress Alexandra* (Westport, Connecticut, Greenwood Press, 1999), p. 388

p. 207 'He spoke . . . with her', Princess Irina Paley, 'Souvenirs de mon père' in Jacques Ferrand, *Le Grand-duc Paul Alexandrovitch de Russie* (Paris, Jacques Ferrand, 1993), p. 12

Chapter 12 – Full Circle

p. 210 'Into our field . . . the cross', *Am Hof des Letzten Zaren*, p. 112

p. 214 'yet heart and soul . . . the movement', quoted in John Wimbles, 'Two Romanov Brides', in *Royalty Digest*, vol. X, no. 8, p. 226. Grand Prince Kirill's birth to a non-Orthodox mother was held against him, as was the manner in which he contracted his own marriage, but most of all he was condemned for his removal of the naval guard detachment from the Alexander Palace while the Tsaritsa and her children were still inside, and for his premature pledge of allegiance to the new powers before the Tsar's abdication, which broke the oath he had already sworn on reaching manhood

p. 215 'I felt proud . . . kiss her', *The Last Grand Duchess*, p. 167

p.218 A wedding on this date is described in family memoirs and listed in genealogies. But an entry from Grand Princess Ksenia's diary, now held in the Hoover Institution, makes it clear that the wedding did not in fact take place until after 13 November, and that the pregnancy had forced Andrei's hand. See John Van Der Kiste and Coryne Hall, *Once a Grand Duchess* (Stroud, Sutton Publishing, 2002), p. 140

p. 219 'We all . . . ceremony', *Memoirs of HRH Prince Christopher of Greece* (London, Right Book Club, 1938), p. 194

Acknowledgements

The position of photographs on the page is indicated by letters: t=top, b=bottom, r=right, l=left.

The Royal Archives © HM Queen Elizabeth II: 6t, 7, 28b, 43t, 44, 67t, 68, 78, 122t, 124t
© Staatsarchiv Darmstadt: 5, 8, 9t, 10 (both), 24 (all), 25 (all), 27t, 28t, 30t, 30tr, 32, 40t, 42t, 45b, 47b, 48, 70tl, 72, 82, 84 (both), 89t, 97 (both), 100, 114t, 126–8 (all), 129t, 130–2 (all), 150b, 152, 171 (all), 172 (both), 174b, 175tr, 177, 189, 190t
The Beinecke Rare Book and Manuscript Library, Yale University: frontispiece, 18t, 80 (both), 110b, 153 (both), 162t, 163t (both), 164bl, 165t & bl, 166 (all), 168 (all), 170t & br, 174t, 175tl & b, 176b, 196t, 198 (both), 199t
Collection of Princess Irina Bagration-Moukhransky: 30b, 46 (both), 47t, 55 (both), 60b, 62 (both), 66b, 74tr, 102b (both), 103t, 105, 150t, 186, 213
Collection of Prince Nicholas and Prince Dimitri Romanoff: 157b, 203, 221b
Nancy Tryon Collection: xiit, xiiitl & br, 4b, 11b, 35t (both), 56b, 74b, 98b, 114b, 119b, 138b, 141, 148, 149 (all), 156b (both), 161tl, 167t, 178b, 180t, 181b, 183b, 192b, 200b, 202t, 205t, 212b, 215b, 216, 217br, 219b (both)
Eric N. Buseyne Collection: 12, 13b, 49 (both), 50b, 63b, 64b, 87, 88t, 106t (both), 117b, 122b, 142tr, 181t, 201t, 205b, 206br, 222t, 225tl & b
Revd T. Mclean Wilson Collection: 38t, 52b, 124b, 144t, 146t & middle, 160t, 176t, 195b, 208br

All other photographs in this book are from the private collections of the author and friends: some preferred not to be identified but still know that I appreciate their help. My special thanks go to Princess Irina Bagration-Moukhransky, to Francis Dimond of the Royal Photograph Collection at Windsor, to Dr E.G. Franz of the Staatsarchiv Darmstadt (and to the Staatsarchiv's excellent photographer), to the staff of the Beinecke Library, Prince Dimitri Romanoff, Ian Shapiro and Argyll Etkin; to Nancy Tryon, Eric Buseyne, David Cripps, the Revd T. Mclean Wilson, Sue Woolmans, Hilde Vieveen, Helen Berger, John Wimbles, Olga Barkovets, Elena Yablochkina, Konstantin Eggert, Bearn Bilker, Katrina Warne, Marion Wynn, Diana de Courcy Ireland, Coryne Hall and Ruth Abrahams for helping to find and identify photographs, for lending interesting photographs, for coming up with documentary material and information and offering encouragement along the way, to Paul Koulikovsky for permission to reproduce the painting by Grand Princess Olga Alexandrovna on page 200 – and not forgetting my agent Sheila Watson, my editors Jaqueline Mitchell and Matthew Brown and my mother, who is thoroughly bored with Romanovs. . . .

Every effort has been made to trace and contact the original owners of all photographs. If copyright has inadvertently been infringed, copyright holders should write to the publisher with full details. Upon copyright being established, a correct credit will be incorporated into future editions of the book.

THE WORK OF THE FOLLOWING PHOTOGRAPHERS IS REPRESENTED

Not all of these attributions will be correct. In the nineteenth century it was not uncommon for one photographer to reproduce the work of another and mount it as his own. Wesenberg of St Petersburg certainly claimed work by Levitsky and Gorodetsky, maybe others, but Russian photographers did not enjoy copyright on their work until the 1890s, so this must have been perfectly legal. Then, later photographers would sometimes re-photograph whole collections of material and print the copies under their own name: Elfelt of Denmark is a prime example, as is J.&J. Bisset of Ballater – both of whom were active in the 1920s and '30s. They did nothing wrong, but the practice makes photographic identification very tricky.

Alexandra Feodorovna, Tsaritsa of Russia, 199b

Alexandrovsko, St Petersburg, 45t

Angerer, L.&V., Vienna, 95b, 96t

Asikritov, Moscow, 137t, 158tr, 188t

Backofen, Damstadt, 2b, 12

Bergamasco, Karl, St Petersburg, 6b, 7, 10b, 45b, 62t, 63t, 71t, 74tl, 77b (both), 81t, 82, 85b, 95t, 97 (both), 105, 135tr, 137b, 155t, 177, 193 (both)

Boissonas & Eggler, St Petersburg , xii (all), xiii (all), 2t, 17b, 19 (all), 20tr, 83t &bl, 101t, 104t, 110t, 158b

Borovitinov, M., 13b

Boucas, George, Athens, 37b

Boute, Brussels, 213

Bulla, Karl, St Petersburg, 139t, 140 (both), 141 (both), 146b

Denier, H., St Petersburg, 43b, 70b

Disderi, Paris, 112b

Downey, W&D, 94br

Elfelt, Copenhagen, 109b, 119b, 120 (both), 121 (both)

Falmotov, 161tl

Fisher, Karl, Moscow, 126, 156b (both) (and Andrianov) 149 (all)

Flormann, Gusta, Stockholm, 86t

Giese, A., Copenhagen, 179t

Gimm, A. Gotha, 107t

Gorodetsky, St Petersburg, 55b, 99 (both; these also appear on Wesenberg mounts)

de Hahn, K.E. (Alexander Yagelsky), St Petersburg, 14b (both), 15b, 17t, 63b, 79t, 128t, 129t

Hanfstaengl, Erwin, Stuttgart, 117t

Hansen, Georg, Copenhagen, 3 (both), 118, 119t, 178t

Hirrlinger, Alfred, Stuttgart, 35tl

Hohlenberg, Copenhagen, 122bl

Hoppé, E.O., 223b

Jasvoin, W., St Petersburg, 15tl, 51b, 58b, 66t, 67b, 71b, 74b

Jurgenson, Berlin, 143t

Kameke, The Hague, 112t

Kersten, Arno, Altenburg, 46t

Laponier, 107b

Lapré, V., Tsarskoe Selo, 49b, 61b, 66b

Levitsky, Sergei (and studio), St Petersburg, vi, 4 (both), 5, 6t, 9b, 10b, 14t, 15tr, 16t, 22, 28b, 32, 33tl, 41 (both), 47t, 58tl, 62b, 65t, 69b, 72, 78b, 89t, 94t & bl, 98b, 100, 134t, 135b, 136t, 152 (both), 158tl, 229

Merlin, Athens, 35tl

Moraites, Athens, 96b

de Mrosovksy, Helen, St Petersburg, 11t

Namahov, A., Yalta, 169b

Nègre, Charles, 180b

Otsup, A., 138b

Pasetti, St Petersburg, 49t, 50 (both), 53, 54t, 55t, 64b, 74tr, 98t, 122br, 144b, 156t, 179b

Ponomareff, I.N., 61t

Sandau, Ernst, Berlin, 143b

Self, 226 (all), 227 (both)

Sock, Oscar, Karlsruhe, 114b

Uhlenhuth, Coburg, 222b

Van Bosch, Wiesbaden, 184b

Verry, Paris, 23 (both), 76 (both)

Vestly, E., Tiflis, 69t, 70tr, 81b

Witte, Hermann, Baden-Baden, 114t

Yagelsky, Alexander – see Hahn, K.E.

Zhukova, P., 73b

The remainder are unidentified in the original.

Index

Members of the imperial family and other reigning families are indexed by Christian name, others by surname.
Page numbers in italics refer to illustrations

Aage of Denmark, Prince, *160*
Abas-Tuman, *181*
Ai-Todor, 169, 218
Alapaevsk, 206
Albert of Belgium, Prince, 99
Albert Victor, Prince, Duke of Clarence and Avondale, *118*, *119*, *120*, *121*
Albrecht of Schaumburg-Lippe, Prince, *117*
Albrecht of Schaumburg-Lippe, Prince (nephew of the above), *117*
Alexander II, Tsar, vii, viii, ix, x, xi, *21*, *22*, *23*, *26*, *33*, 40, 41, 45, 71, 81, 84, *94*, *134*, 151, 173, 177, 185, *187*, 192
Alexander III, Tsar, x, *3*, 4, 13, 21, *22*, *24*, 27, 30, *34*, 37, 48, 51, 58, 62, 70, *76*, 86, *120*, *136*, 137, 149, 152, *173*, 177, *183*, 185, 193, *229*
Alexander Alexandrovich, Grand Prince, 5, 178
Alexander Mikhailovich, Grand Prince, *xiii*, 6, *38*, 47, 71, *86*, *98*, *158*, 160, 169, 182, 210, 225
Alexander Lyceum, Tsarskoe Selo, 78, 79
Alexander of Schaumburg-Lippe, Prince, *117*
Alexander Palace, Tsarskoe Selo, xiv, 4, 6, 14, 18, 59, 127, *162*, 174, 189, 205, *226*
Alexander, Crown Prince of Serbia, later King of Yugoslavia, 110
Alexander, Prince of Bulgaria (Prince Alexander of Battenberg), *192*
Alexandra Alexandrovna, Grand Princess, 178
Alexandra Feodorovna, Tsaritsa, wife of Nicholas I (Princess Charlotte of Prussia), viii, *40*
Alexandra Feodorovna, Tsaritsa, wife of Nicholas II (Princess Alix of Hesse), *2*, *9*, *10*, *12*, *13*, *14*, *15*, *16*, *18*, *20*, 53, 54, *124*, *125*, *130*, *133*, *139*, *140*, *141*, *142*, *144*, *147*, *150*, *153*, *158*, *160*, *161*, *163*, *164*, *165*, *166*, *168*, *171*, *174*, *175*, *176*, *198*, *203*, *204*, 228
Alexandra Georgievna, Grand Princess Pavel (Princess of Greece), *49*, *50*, *101*, *179*
Alexandra Iosifovna, Grand Princess Konstantin (Princess of Saxe-Altenburg), x, *34*, *41*, *43*, *50*, *95*, *101*, 105, 145, 155, 182, *184*
Alexandra of Cumberland, Princess, *121*
Alexandra of Saxe-Coburg, Princess, *116*
Alexandra Petrovna, Grand Princess Konstantin (Princess of Oldenburg), *31*, *43*, 55
Alexandra, Queen of Great Britain (Princess of Wales), *3*, 65, *119*, *120*, 124, *125*
Alexandria Peterhof, 7, 16, 67, *168*, *226*
Alexandrine, Queen of Denmark, *115*
Alexei Alexandrovich, Grand Prince, x, *22*, *25*, 59, *76*, *84*, 85, *137*, 167, *194*
Alexei Mikhailovich, Grand Prince, *34*, *182*
Alexei Nikolaevich, Grand Prince Tsesarevich, *frontispiece*, *2*, *16*, *17*, *18*, *20*, 59, *60*, 80, *83*, 109, 127, *128*, *129*, 141, 151, 153, 161, *162*, *163*, *164*, *165*, *166*, *168*, *170*, *172*, *174*, *175*, 199, *203*, 205, *226*, 228
Alfred of Saxe-Coburg, Prince, *94*
Alfred, Prince, Duke of Saxe-Coburg, *94*, 192
Alice, Princess, Grand Duchess of Hesse and by Rhine, 8, 9

Almedingen, E. A., vii, 59
Anastasia Mikhailovna, Grand Princess, Grand Duchess of Mecklenburg-Schwerin, *31*, *37*, *69*, *97*, *115*, *145*, *222*
Anastasia Nikolaevna, Grand Princess, *2*, *16*, *18*, *19*, 60, *110*, *125*, *128*, *151*, *160*, *163*, *168*, *170*, *171*, *175*, *199*, *203*, *205*, 228
Anastasia Nikolaevna, 'Stana', Grand Princess Nikolai (Princess of Montenegro), *51*, *167*, *202*, *209*, *212*
Andreas (Andrew) of Greece, Prince, 125, 129, 223
Andrei Alexandrovich, Prince, *38*, *54*, *61*, *73*, *160*, *169*, *218*, *219*, 237
Andrei Vladimirovich, Grand Prince, *34*, *47*, *62*, 65, *108*, *159*
Angermanland, Swedish ship, 213
Anichkov Palace, 7, 104
Anna Pavlovna, Grand Princess, Queen of the Netherlands, 112
Arthur, Prince, Duke of Connaught, *125*
Axel of Denmark, Prince, *160*
Audrey, Princess Romanovsky-Ilinsky (Audrey Emery), *217*
Augusta, Kaiserin (Princess of Saxe-Weimar), *113*
Augusta Viktoria, Kaiserin (Princess of Schleswig-Holstein-Augustenburg), *142*

Bagration-Mukhransky, Prince Konstantin, *102*
Bagration-Mukhransky, Princess Nathalie, *103*, *213*
Bagration-Mukhransky, Prince Teymuraz, *102*, *103*, *213*
Baltazzi, Mme, *150*
Bariatinsky, Prince Alexander, *224*
Bathildis of Schaumburg-Lippe, Princess, *117*
Bazhanov, Father, 193
Beatrice of Saxe-Coburg, Princess, 109, *116*
Beatrix, Queen of the Netherlands, 112
Bernhard of Saxe-Weimar, Prince, *113*
Berthold of Baden, Prince, *114*
Bestuzhev-Ryumin, Prince, 76
Boissonas & Eggler, x, xii
Boris Vladimirovich, Grand Prince, *34*, *47*, *54*, *62*, 65, 186, 194, *204*
Brasov, George, *109*
Brasova, Natalia (née Sheremetevskaya), *109*
Burenina, Sophie, 51
Burton Holmes, E., 137
Buxhoeveden, Baroness Sophie, 16, 17, *147*, 153, 156
Byttin, Dr., *182*

Carl Alexander, Grand Duke of Saxe-Weimar, *113*
Carl August, Hereditary Grand Duke of Saxe-Weimar, *113*
Carol I, King of Romania (Prince Karl of Hohenzollern-Sigmaringen), *142*, 192
Carol of Romania, Prince (later King Carol II), 110
Carrick, William, x, 2
Catherine II, 'the Great', 39, 96
Cecile of Greece, Princess, *223*
Cecilie, Crown Princess of Prussia (Princess of Mecklenburg-Schwerin), *115*, *222*
Charles Edward, Duke of Saxe-Coburg, *116*

Chivelev, Professor, 76
Christian IX, King of Denmark, *3*, 59, 95, *124*, *183*
Christian X, King of Denmark, *115*, *119*
Christian of Cumberland, Prince, *121*
Christoph of Hesse-Cassel, Prince, 223
Christopher of Greece, Prince, *111*, *121*, 125
Cody, 'Buffalo' Bill, 85
Constantine I, King of the Hellenes, *96*, *120*, *121*, *125*
Contrexéville, 167, 215
Court dress, 91, 144
Crimea, 31
Crofts, Millicent, 65
Custer, George Armstrong, 85

Daguerre, Louis, vii, viii
Dauthendey, Karl, viii
Denier, Andrei, ix, x
Denier, H., x
Derevenko, Andrei Eremeievich, *128*, *170*
Djulber, 209
Dmitri Alexandrovich, Prince, *38*, *73*, *211*, *219*
Dmiti Konstantinovich, Grand Prince, 30, *35*, *43*, 71, 74, 186, 187, *208*
Dmitri Pavlovich, Grand Prince, *57*, *64*, *83*, *104*, 110, *125*, *126*, *172*, *179*, 188, *189*, 217
Dmitri Romanoff, Prince, *221*
Dolgoruky, Prince Sergei, 211
Dolgoruky, Princess Sophie, *211*
Dostoevsky, Feodor, x, 77
Drentein, Captain, *170*

Eadie, Lilian, *128*
Eagar, Margaretta, 67, 124
Edward VII, King of Great Britain (Prince of Wales), *3*, 124, *125*
Ekaterina Ioannovna, Princess, 213
Ekaterina Mikhailovna, Grand Princess, Duchess Georg of Mecklenburg-Strelitz, 187
Ekaterina Pavlovna, Grand Princess, Princess of Württemberg, 112
Ekaterinburg, 205, 206, 213
Elena of Leuchtenberg, 157
Elena Pavlovna, Grand Princess, Hereditary Grand Duchess of Mecklenburg-Schwerin, 113, 115
Elena Pavlovna, Grand Princess Mikhail (Princess Charlotte of Württemberg), *40*, 135
Elena Petrovna, Princess Ioann (Princess of Serbia), *56*, 213
Elena, Queen of Italy, 56
Elena Vladimirovna, Grand Princess, Princess Nicholas of Greece, *34*, *47*, *54*, 65, *90*, *93*, *99*, *123*, 125, *145*
Elisabeta of Romania, Princess (later Queen of the Hellenes), 103
Elisabeth of Hesse, Princess, *125*
Elisabeth, Princess Johann Albrecht of Mecklenburg-Schwerin (Princess of Saxe-Weimar), *113*
Elizabeth of Greece, Princess, *123*
Elizabeth, Queen, The Queen Mother, 199
Elizaveta Feodorovna, 'Ella', Grand Princess Sergei (Princess Elisabeth of Hesse), *8*, *10*,

14, *47, 48, 49, 101, 125, 126, 130, 132, 149, 157, 158,* 179, *188, 189, 190, 207, 209, 227*
Elizaveta Mavrikievna, Grand Princess Konstantin (Princess of Saxe-Altenburg), *39, 46, 55, 62, 79, 145, 150, 178,* 185, 186, *213*
Elizaveta, Princess Andrei Romanoff (Elizaveta di Friderici, née di Sasso-Ruffo), *218*
Elsa, Princess Albrecht of Schaumburg-Lippe (Princess of Württemberg), 29, *117, 145*
Erik of Denmark, Prince, *160*
Ernst II, Duke of Saxe-Altenburg, *55*
Ernst August of Cumberland, Prince, *121*
Ernst August, Duke of Cumberland, 121
Ernst Ludwig, Grand Duke of Hesse and by Rhine, 8, *9,* 10, *12, 47,* 107, *125, 127, 130, 131, 132,* 150, *171,* 189
Eugen of Schaumburg-Lippe, Prince, *117*

Fane, Mr., 98
Feodor Alexandrovich, Prince, *38, 73, 211,* 218, *219*
Ferdinand, King of Bulgaria, 99
Fox Talbot, Henry, *viii*
Franklin, Mrs Elizabeth, 65
Franz Josef of Schaumburg-Lippe, Prince, *117*
Fredericks, Count, *160, 170, 194*
Frederik VIII, King of Denmark, *3,* 119
Frederik IX, King of Denmark, *115*
Friedburg, *128, 129*
Friedrich Franz III, Grand Duke of Mecklenburg-Schwerin, 97
Friedrich Franz IV, Grand Duke of Mecklenburg-Schwerin, *115,* 222
Friedrich Karl of Hesse-Cassel, Prince, 125
Fry, Mrs Frances, *64*

Gatchina, 21, 90
Gavril Konstantinovich, Prince, *55, 62, 79, 88,* 186, *225*
Georg Donatus of Hesse, Hereditary Prince, *128, 129,* 223
Georg Wilhelm of Cumberland, Prince, *121*
George I, King of the Hellenes, 95, *96,* 119, *125*
George of Battenberg, Prince, *125*
George of Greece, Prince, *96, 119, 121, 122, 125*
George V, King of Great Britain (George, Duke of York), 59, *118, 119, 143,* 223
Georgi Alexandrovich, Grand Prince Tsesarevich, *6, 7, 27, 61, 72, 78, 119, 120, 121,* 151, *181,* 229
Georgi Konstantinovich, Prince, *55, 60, 73, 213*
Georgi Mikhailovich, Grand Prince, *37,* 52, 71, *125, 159,* 186, *208*
Georgi, Duke of Leuchtenberg, 51
Golitsina, Princess, 58, 59
Gottfried of Hohenlohe-Langenburg, Prince, 223
Grove, Elizabeth, *64*
Gustav V, King of Sweden, *142*

Haakon, King of Norway (Prince Carl of Denmark), *125*
Hammel, I., vii, viii
Harax, *172*
Heath, Charles, 78
Heinrich of Mecklenburg-Schwerin, Prince, Prince Hendrik of the Netherlands, 112
Heinrich of Prussia, Prince, *125, 132*
Heinrich VII, Prince Reuss, *113*
Helena Victoria of Schleswig-Holstein, *125*
Hélène of Orleans, Princess, *11*
Hélène of Mecklenburg-Strelitz, Princess Albert of Saxe-Altenburg, *145*
Hilda of Anhalt Dessau, Princess, *3*

Ignatiev, Countess, 106
Igor Konstantinovich, Prince, *55,* 60, *66, 79, 138, 206*
Ilinskoe, 10, *126,* 179, *189*
Ioann Konstantinovich, Prince, *55, 56,* 59, *62, 79, 88,* 186, *206*
Irina Alexandrovna, Princess, *xii, xiii,* 38, *60, 61, 73, 98, 104, 168, 169, 219*
Irène of Hesse, Princess, Princess Heinrich of Prussia, 9, 106, *125, 130*

Jasvoin, W., x
Johann Albrecht of Mecklenburg Schwerin, Prince, *113*
'Joy' (Tsesarevich Alexei's spaniel), *199*
Julius of Glücksburg, Prince, *3*

Karelin, Andrei, x
Karl of Leiningen, Prince, *219*
Karl of Württemberg, Hereditary Prince (later King), 29
Kharkov, 184
Kira Kirillovna, Princess, *190*
Kirill Vladimirovich, Grand Prince, *45, 47, 54,* 65, *86,* 107, *116,* 182, 186, *194,* 237
Klein, Angelika, 66
Kleinmichel, Olga, 188
Knebworth, 109
Knud of Denmark, Prince, *115*
Konstantin Konstantinovich, Grand Prince, xiv, 15, *30, 34, 35, 43, 46, 55,* 60, *62, 74, 77, 79, 85, 138,* 150, *155, 156,* 157, *167,* 182, *185, 186*
Konstantin Konstantinovich, Prince, *55, 66, 74, 79, 103,* 110, *138, 156,* 186, *204*
Konstantin Nikolaevich, Grand Prince, viii, *30,* 40, 41, 43, 84, 85, *135,* 155, 182, *185*
Kodovsky, Professor, 154
Korotchenzov, Alexander, 213
Kossikovskaya, Alexandra, 109
Krasnoe Selo, 11, 34, 146
Kremlin, Moscow, 188, 213, 227
Ksenia Alexandrovna, Grand Princess, *xii, xiii,* xiv, 7, *27, 34,* 38, *44,* 60, *63, 65,* 69, *98, 119,* 122, *158,* 160, *219,* 229
Ksenia Georgievna, Princess, Mrs William Leeds, *37, 52, 219*
Kschessinskaya, Mathilde, *11,* 38: with her son Vladimir, 'Vova', later known as Prince Romanovsky-Krasinsky, *108,* 215
Kulikovsky, Guri, *216*
Kulikovsky, Tihon, *216*
Kulikovsky, Nikolai, 200, *216*

Leeds, William, *219*
Lennart, Prince, *101*
Leonid, Abbot, 77
Leopold of Battenberg, Prince, *116*
Leopold, Prince, Duke of Albany, 174
Levitsky, Sergei, x, 22
Litke, Admiral Feodor, 30
Livadia, Crimea, 6, 13, 27, *169, 170, 172,* 174, 183
Londonderry, Lady, 40
Louise Margaret, Duchess of Connaught, *125, 145*
Louise, Queen of Sweden (Princess of Battenberg), *125*
Louise of Denmark, Princess, *119*
Louise of Wales, Princess, 106, *119, 121, 125*
Louise, Queen of Denmark (wife of Christian 1X), *3, 119, 183*
Louise, Queen of Denmark (wife of Frederik VIII), *119*
Ludwig IV, (Louis) Grand Duke of Hesse and by Rhine, 8, *10,* 47

Ludwig of Hesse, Prince, *128, 129, 131*
Luise, Grand Duchess of Baden (Princess of Prussia), 113

Makarov, Admiral, 194
Marble Palace, 213, 225
Margaret of Connaught, Princess, *125*
Margarita of Greece, Princess, *129, 223*
Maria Alexandrovna, Grand Princess, Duchess of Edinburgh and Saxe-Coburg, 22, 25, 28, *68, 89, 92, 94,* 102, 103, *116, 177,* 222
Maria Alexandrovna, Tsaritsa, wife of Alexander II (Princess Marie of Hesse), viii, ix, xi, *22, 23,* 26, *28, 32, 41,* 57, *89, 152, 177,* 193
Maria Feodorovna, Tsaritsa, wife of Alexander III (Princess Dagmar of Denmark), x, xi, xiv, *3, 4, 6, 7,* 11, *12, 13,* 14, *22, 27, 34, 44,* 45, 50, *53, 54,* 63, *90, 95, 97, 98,* 100, *104, 119, 120, 139, 144,* 160, *178,* 180, 209, *210, 220,* 229
Maria Georgievna, Grand Princess Georgi (Princess Marie of Greece), 38, *52,* 89, 101, *122, 125, 201*
Maria Kirillovna, Princess, Princess Carl of Leiningen, *107, 219*
Maria Nikolaevna, Grand Princess, 2, *15, 17, 18, 19,* 58, *67, 125, 128,* 160, *165, 168, 169, 170, 171, 175, 199, 203, 205, 228*
Maria Nikolaevna, Grand Princess, Duchess of Leuchtenberg, viii, *29,* 136
Maria Pavlovna, Grand Princess, Grand Duchess Carl Alexander of Saxe-Weimar, 113
Maria Pavlovna the elder, Grand Princess Vladimir (Duchess of Mecklenburg-Schwerin), *34, 45, 47, 54,* 97, *99,* 107, *108,* 115, *145,* 152, *167, 190, 201,* 204, *215*
Maria Pavlovna the younger, Grand Princess, Princess Vilhelm of Sweden, Princess Putiatin, *50, 58, 61, 64, 91, 101, 125, 179, 188, 189, 207, 225*
Maria, Princess Romanovsky, Duchess of Leuchtenberg, Princess Wilhelm of Baden, *114*
Marie Alexandra of Baden, Princess, *114*
Marie Louise, Princess Max of Baden (Princess of Cumberland), 114
Marie, Princess Friedrich of Anhalt-Dessau, *3*
Marie, Princess Reuss (Princess of Saxe-Weimar), *113*
Marie, Queen of Romania, *94, 116*
Marina of Greece, Princess, *123*
Marina Petrovna, Princess, *66,* 71, *154,* 157, 203, *212*
Marlborough, HMS, *210, 211, 212*
Marling, Sir Charles and Lady, 217
Martha and Mary Convent, Moscow, 132, 189, 190, 227
Massandra, Crimea, *168*
Maud of Wales, Princess (Queen of Norway), *119, 125*
Max of Schaumburg-Lippe, Prince, *117*
Maximilian, 3rd Duke of Leuchtenberg, viii, 29
Maximilian of Baden, Prince, *93, 99,* 114
Maximilian of Schaumburg-Lippe, Prince, 117
Merenberg, Count Georg, 224
Mescherskaya, Princess Marie Elimovna, 3
Michael Romanoff, Prince, *218*
Mikhail Alexandrovich, Grand Prince, xiv, 7, *27, 34, 44,* 63, *78,* 109, 116, *119,* 159, *160,* 182, *183,* 205
Mikhail Mikhailovich, Grand Prince, *37,* 70, *106, 114,* 184, *223*
Mikhail Nikolaevich, Grand Prince, viii, *31, 34,* 42, *98,* 115, *135,* 136, *159, 161*

Mikhail Pavlovich, Grand Prince, viii, 40
Militsa Nikolaevna, Grand Princess Peter
    (Princess of Montenegro), *51*, 209, *212*
Milord (Alexander II's dog), xi, *33*
Molchanov, Mascha, 66
Molchanov, Maxim, 66
Mountbatten, Lord Louis, 126, *128*

Nadejda Petrovna, Princess, *157*, *203*, *212*
Natalia Konstantinovna, Princess, 177
Nelson, HMS, *212*
Nice, *180*
Nicholas I, Tsar, viii, ix, 21, 39, 40, 41, 57, 84
Nicholas II, Tsar, *frontispiece*, *vi*, vii, x, xix, *1*, *2*, *4*, *5*, *6*,
    7, *8*, *9*, *12*, *13*, *14*, *16*, 20, 21, *22*, 27, *34*, 51, 58,
    61, *72*, *78*, *80*, 87, 88, 102, 107, *111*, 112, *118*,
    119, *120*, *121*, *122*, *124*, *125*, *127*, *133*, *137*,
    139, *140*, *141*, *142*, *143*, *146*, *147*, 151, *157*,
    158, *160*, *161*, *162*, *163*, *164*, *165*, *171*, *172*,
    176, *178*, 186, *191*, *194*, 195, *196*, *226*, *228*, *229*
Nicholas of Greece, Prince, *99*, 123
Nicholas Romanoff, Prince, *221*
Niépce, Isidore, viii, 233
Nikita Alexandrovich, Prince, *38*, *73*, *211*, 218,
    219
Nikola I, King of Montenegro, 51
Nikolai Alexandrovich, Grand Prince
    Tsesarevich, ix, *2*, *3*, *24*, 30, 44, 57, *76*, *180*
Nikolai Konstantinovich, Grand Prince, *30*,
    34, *43*, 84, 85, *105*
Nikolai Mikhailovich, Grand Prince, *31*, *36*,
    81, *114*, 186, *208*
Nikolai Nikolaevich the elder, Grand Prince
    (son of Nicholas I), viii, x, *31*, 43, *135*, *192*
Nikolai Nikolaevich the younger, Grand Prince
    (son of the above), *31*, *34*, *36*, 51, 66, *81*,
    140, *161*, *167*, 195, *196*, *202*, 209, 210, *212*
Nilov, Admiral, *160*
Nina Georgievna, Princess, *37*, *52*, *172*

Oath of Allegiance, 8, 21
Oleg Konstantinovich, Prince, *55*, 66, *74*, *75*,
    79, *138*, 178, *197*, 203
Olga Alexandrovna, Grand Princess, Duchess
    Peter of Oldenburg, Mrs. Kulikovsky, *xii*,
    xiii, 7, 27, *63*, 67, *65*, 90, 91, 92, *100*, *119*,
    120, *124*, *148*, 154, *160*, *168*, *169*, *200*
Olga Feodorovna, Grand Princess Mikhail
    (Princess Cäcilie of Baden), *31*, *42*, 69, 114,
    184
Olga Konstantinovna, Grand Princess, Queen
    of the Hellenes, *30*, *34*, *35*, *43*, 49, *50*, 88,
    95, *96*, *101*, 105, *125*, 150, *155*, 213, 223
Olga Nikolaevna, Grand Princess, *2*, *14*, *15*,
    17, *18*, *19*, *53*, *74*, *110*, *125*, *127*, *130*, *141*,
    153, *160*, *164*, *198*, *203*, 204, 215, *228*
Olga Nikolaevna, Grand Princess, Queen of
    Württemberg, viii, *29*, 41, 57, *89*, 117
Olga of Cumberland, Princess, *121*
Olga of Greece, Princess, *123*
Olga, Princess Maximilian of Schaumburg-
    Lippe (Princess of Württemberg, *29*, *117*
Oom, Feodor, 3
Orlov, Princess Irina, *212*
Orlov, Prince Nikolai, 203

Paley, Prince Vladimir, *106*, 207
Paley, Princess Irina, *106*, 207
Paley, Princess Natalia, *106*
Paley, Princess Olga (née Karnovich), *106*, 207
Pasetti, A.A., x
Patricia of Connaught, Princess, *125*
Paul I, Tsar, 15

Paul Friedrich of Mecklenburg-Schwerin,
    Duke, 115
Paul, Prince Romanovsky-Ilinsky, *217*
Pauline, Hereditary Grand Duchess of Saxe-
    Weimar, *113*
Pavel Alexandrovich, Grand Prince, *21*, *22*, *26*, *28*,
    32, *34*, *49*, 71, *82*, 89, *106*, *152*, 177, *179*, 207
Peter Nikolaevich, Grand Prince, xiv, 31, *36*,
    51, 66, *71*, 203, 209, *212*, 220
Peter of Oldenburg, Duke, *34*, *100*, 200
Petropavlovsk, Russian naval ship, 194
Petrov, Piotr Vasilievich, *80*
Philip, Prince, Duke of Edinburgh, 129, *223*
Piazzi Smyth, Charles, ix
Pless, Princess of, 97
    'Popka' (Georgi Alexadnrovich's parrot), 78
Prascovia, Princess Roman (Countess
    Prascovia Sheremetev), *221*
Prokudin-Gorskii, Sergei, xiv
Provender, Kent, 218
Pushkin, Alexander, 79, 106
Putiatin, Prince Sergei Mikhailovich, 207

Repin, Ilya, 149
Röhmer, Mademoiselle, vii
Roman Petrovich, Prince, vii, *66*, *71*, 154, *157*,
    176, *203*, 210, *212*, 218, *220*
Rostislav Alexandrovich, Prince, x, *38*, *73*, *211*, *219*
Rubinstein, Anton, 22, 25

St Peter and St Paul, Cathedral and Fortress, St
    Petersburg, 173, 208
Sergei Alexandrovich, Grand Prince, 8, *22*, 25,
    28, *32*, *34*, *47*, 48, 49, 50, 64, *68*, 70, 76, 77,
    89, *125*, *137*, *139*, *152*, 155, *158*, 179, *188*,
    193, 227
Sergei Mikhailovich, Grand Prince, *34*, *38*, 42,
    70, 108, *206*
Sergei, Prince Romanovsky, Duke of
    Leuchtenberg, *193*
Shishkin, Ivan, x
Shtandart, imperial yacht, *131*, *153*, *164*, *165*,
Smolny Institute, 33, 51, 56
Sophie of Greece, Princess, *223*
Sophie, Grand Duchess of Saxe-Weimar
    (Princess of the Netherlands), *113*
Sophie, Queen of the Hellenes (Princess of
    Prussia), *125*
Sophie, Queen of the Netherlands, 112
Spiridonov, Ekaterina, 66
Spiridovich, Alexander, 139
Stanley, Lady Augusta, 85, 89
Stahl, Maria, 212
Stasov, Vladimir, ix
Stead, W.T., 78, 112
Stopford, Albert, 201
Strauss, Johann, 155
Strelna, 186
Stroganov, Count Grigori, 29
Strutton, Kitty, 68
Sukhomlinov, General, Minister of War, *202*
Suvorov, Prince, *192*
Svetlana, Russian naval frigate, 85

Tashkent, 105
Tatiana Konstantinovna, Princess, Princess
    Konstantin Bagration-Mukhransky, *55*, 66,
    74, *79*, *91*, *92*, *102*, 150, *213*
Tatiana Nikolaevna, Grand Princess, *2*, *14*, *15*,
    17, *18*, *19*, 67, *74*, *91*, *92*, *110*, *124*, *125*,
    131, *141*, 156, *160*, *164*, *168*, *169*, *198*,
    203, *205*, 228
Taylor, Mrs, 66
Thaddeus Jones, Henry, 90

Theodora of Greece, Princess, *129*, *223*
Thormeyer, Ferdinand, 78
Thyra, of Denmark, Princess, Duchess of
    Cumberland, *3*, *119*, 121
Tiutcheva, Anna, 41
Tiutcheva, Mme., *160*
Tolstoy, Countess Alexandra, 68
Torby, Countess Anastasia, Lady 'Zia' Wehrner,
    106, 223
Torby, Count Michael, *223*
Torby, Countess Nadejda, Marchioness of
    Milford Haven, *106*, 223
Torby, Countess Sophie (née Merenberg), *37*, *106*
Tsarevna, yacht, 182,
Turgenev, Dr, 179

Valdemar of Denmark, Prince, *3*, *119*
Vasili Alexandrovich, Prince, *xii*, *xiii*, *38*, *211*, *219*
Vasnetsov, Victor, 153, 227
Vera Konstantinovna, Grand Princess, Duchess
    Wilhelm Eugen of Württemberg, 29, *30*,
    35, *43*, *105*, *125*, *145*
Vera Konstantinovna, Princess, *55*, *60*, *89*, *117*,
    185, *213*
Viacheslav Konstantinovich, Grand Prince, 30,
    74, 77, *182*
Victoria Adelheid, Duchess of Saxe-Coburg, *116*
Victoria Melita of Edinburgh and Saxe-
    Coburg, Princess, Grand Duchess of Hesse,
    Grand Princess Kyrill, *12*, *94*, *107*, *116*,
    214
Victoria of Wales, Princess, *119*, *122*, *125*
Victoria, Princess Louis of Battenberg
    (Princess of Hesse), *125*, *126*, *130*
Victoria, Queen of Great Britain, 42, 71
Viktoria of Baden, Princess, Queen of
    Sweden, 114, 213
Vilhelm of Sweden, Prince, *101*, *142*
Vishniakova, Maria, *128*
Vladimir Alexandrovich, Grand Prince, x, *3*,
    22, *24*, *28*, *34*, *45*, *47*, 51, *54*, *76*, *136*, *142*,
    161, 190
Vladimir Kirillovich, Prince, *214*, *215*
Volkov, Alexei, 49, 179
Voronov, Pavel, *110*
Vorres, Ian, 100
Vsevelod Ioannovich, Prince, *59*, 213

Wilhelm, Landgraf of Hesse-Cassel, *3*
Wilhelm Eugen, Duke of Württemberg, *117*
Wilhelm I, Kaiser, 113
Wilhelm II, Kaiser, 59, 113, 137, *143*
Wilhelm of Baden, Prince, 114
Wilhelm Ernst of Saxe-Weimar, Prince, *113*
Wilhelmina, Queen of the Netherlands, *112*
Willem III, King of the Netherlands, *112*
Winter Palace, 8, 13, 40, 42, 94, 95, 187
Wolfsgarten, *129*
Wulfert, Vladimir, 109

Xenia Romanoff, Princess, *218*

Yagelsky, Alexander ('Hahn'), xi
Yourievsky, Princess Catherine, *224*
Yurievskaya, Princess Ekaterina (Princess
    Dolgorukaya), *33*, 173, 187, *224*
Yurievskaya, Princess Olga, Countess Georg
    von Merenberg, *224*
Yurievsky, Prince Georgi, 208
Yusupov, Prince Felix, *104*
Yusupova, Zinaida, 104

Zabavu (yacht), 84
Zagorsk, Toy Museum, 63